D0937674

DIGITIZE OR DIE

DIGITIZE OR DIE

Transform your organization

Embrace the digital evolution

Rise above the competition

Nicolas Windpassinger

Copyright © 2017 Nicolas Windpassinger

All rights reserved. No part of this publication may be reproduced, stored in a retrieval system, or transmitted in any form or by any means, electronic, mechanical, photocopying, recording, scanning, or otherwise, except as permitted under Section 107 or 108 of the 1976 United States Copyright Act, without the prior written permission of the Author.

Limit of Liability/Disclaimer of Warranty; While the publisher and author have used their best efforts in preparing this book, they make no representations or warranties with respect to the accuracy or completeness of the contents of this book and specifically disclaim any implied warranties of merchantability or fitness for a particular purpose. No warranty may be created or extended by sales representatives or written sales materials. The advice and strategies contained herein may not be suitable for your situation. You should consult with a professional where appropriate. The fact that an organization or Web site is referred to in this work as a citation and/or a potential source of further information does not mean that the author or the publisher endorses the information the organization or website may provide or recommendations it may have. Further, readers should be aware that Internet websites listed in this work may have changed or disappeared between when this work was written and when it is read. Neither the publisher nor author shall be liable for any loss of profit or any other commercial damages, including but not limited to special, incidental, consequential, or other damages.

Author: Nicolas Windpassinger
Cover Artist: Maxime Zoffoli
Copy Editor: Richard Lowe, Jr
Publisher: IoT Hub

Author website: :www.nicolaswindpassinger.com

ISBN: 979-10-97580-04-9 (Color Paperback)
ISBN: 979-10-97580-03-2 (Black & White Paperback)
ISBN: 979-10-97580-01-8 (eBook)

DEDICATION

First, a gratitude to all you seekers who want to learn, may you find much more than you're looking for. If this book changes just one life, then it was worth the effort and passion it took me to put it into your hands.

Second, all benefits will be donated to these worthwhile causes:

- Alzheimer's Association (www.alz.org), which provides care and support for all those affected by Alzheimer's and other dementias

- Fondation de France (www.fondationdefrance.org), which supports projects in complex fields, such as education, research and social integration

Third, to Jean-Pascal Tricoire, Chairman & CEO of Schneider Electric for his inspiring foreword.

Fourth, to Olivier Hersent, Chairman & CTO of Actility and Don Tapscott, author of Wikinomics & Blockchain Revolution for their inspiring perspectives.

Finally, to Emilie, whose patience made this book a reality. To Ethan and Emma whose impatience made each written page an adventure.

Table of Contents

FOREWORD

UNLOCKING THE ENERGY DEADLOCK

We are in an energy deadlock: stuck between energy consumption that will increase by 50% over the next 40 years and the urgency to divide global carbon emissions by a factor of two. More energy is being consumed as we urbanize, industrialize, and digitize to drive progress. We discovered with acuity in the past decade, however, that energy is the biggest source of carbon emissions and that they threaten the balance of the very fragile asset we all share: our planet.

We, at Schneider Electric, refuse to live between this rock and hard place and are committed to the indisputable right of everybody on our planet to have access to energy, as energy is the basis of any progress. Yet about 2 billion people today still cannot realize that fundamental right. With energy comes liberation from laborious work, as well as improved education and healthcare. We, at Schneider Electric, support underprivileged communities around the world to escape poverty by closing the energy gap through access to green energy. In both developing and mature economies, we have a conviction to ensure that Life Is On™ everywhere, for everyone, and at every moment. Life Is On when energy is on.

In the face of this Energy Deadlock comes some good news. Renewable energies are reaching parity with other sources, and are taking a significant share of the energy consumption mix. Their deployment is essential for the world's decarbonization. Important improvements on the side of efficiency, however, are necessary for making this transition possible. The Internet of Things is already improving the way we consume, produce, distribute and even share energy; our world is fast becoming very different for our children. It will be more electric, more digitalized, decentralized, and radically more decarbonized. Our generation must take on the climate challenge conundrum and its associated energy deadlock for a better future. For the first time, we have the technologies, the expertise, and the political support to solve the energy paradox. It is up to each one of us, now, to create the new energy world our children will inherit and drive forward.

Digitization is the main catalyst for change. The first wave of the Internet connected people with people, revolutionizing the way we live and engage with each other. The second wave is about connecting people with machines and machines to machines; it is happening now at an unprecedented scale and speed. This pervasive and exponential connectivity — combined with mobility, cloud, sensing, artificial intelligence, and cyber security — will change profoundly the way we live and interact with our environment. It will unleash a flow of data that has never been experienced. In turn, this transformation will enable the whole energy value chain of stakeholders and businesses to better serve their customers by providing more relevant answers to concrete business issues and challenges.

At Schneider Electric, we support the digital transformation of our customers and partners through continuous innovations in converged technologies to increase efficiency and agility, and enable new business models. We bench test our technologies on ourselves. We are on a promising track to become carbon neutral by 2030.

Nicolas's book is all about the Internet of Things (IoT). Not only is it about IoT technologies; it traces how the IoT is changing the way companies must operate in the coming decades to survive and thrive with redesigned strategies, go-to markets, and portfolios. Nicolas suggests that some companies will see change as a threat and, accordingly, will decide to stick to their historical, profitable business models. Others, by contrast, will embrace digitization as an important and essential disruption to core business as usual.

As we know at Schneider Electric, the starting point to any change is understanding the rules of the game. That's what Nicolas clarifies throughout Digitize or Die, writing as a practitioner who has been working on facing this challenge with creativity, innovation, and pragmatism. Many of us at Schneider Electric have adopted this same approach with purpose and passion.

Together with our customers, peers, and partners, we can push way past this energy deadlock. We must start today.

Jean-Pascal Tricoire is the Chairman and CEO of Schneider Electric.

INTRODUCTION

"Smart business people succeed because they get the advice in advance. They find out what the rules of the game are and structure accordingly"
Paul Jacobs

Choosing the title of a book is always one of the most important and challenging tasks—as it was most certainly for me. My dilemma was: How to impart the urgency and the significance of this technological era, so critical, demanding, and fast-moving?

Digitize or Die: It may sound overly dramatic or cliché, however it is simply the reality.

If you don't know the rules of the game, if you don't spend time learning them, how can you expect to win?

If you don't think about adapting, please certainly forget about succeeding. Your worry is going to be about surviving.

MY COMMITMENT TO YOU - FILLING YOUR DIGITAL GAP

Initially, I did not set out to write a book. I had merely wanted to find such a book, but instead discovered it did not exist. I did find a lot of commercial and marketing books but very often with a lack of strategic guidance, or anecdotal reference to what companies are facing. None of the technology books and blogs expanded on the IoT, beyond the pure technology element, in a way that would help companies understand how to transform, leverage themselves and supersede their competition.

I have witnessed so much confusion and trepidation around the IoT with more questions than answers.

The big purpose of this book is to explain the new rules of the game and give simple and pragmatic steps to not only survive but succeed with digital transformation, to provide you with the essential knowledge to understand these new rules.

My commitment here is to be your coach, to guide you and help you understand what the IoT may hold for you, as well as define a digitization strategy so you can put together an action plan to adapt and succeed.

If you commit to stay with me throughout this book, I promise to give you the knowledge to understand what lies behind the fancy acronyms and digital mirage. I will give you a simple, step by step method to assess where your current portfolio is today but more importantly what needs to be done to digitize it.

With my background as a telecom engineer, major account sales, branch manager, channel manager, global channel program manager, and even a start-up venture, I've lived through many of these transformations. Indeed, one of the reasons I've written this book is to share with others what I have learned along with my insights about what might be important coming, just around the corner.

I have seen analog companies disappear, others merely survive, and some hurdle forward of their competition in markets such as the analog telephony to IP switch between 2000 and 2010, the video switch from analog to IP, and the current digitization of homes and energy/power networks. I saw companies that were analog leaders de-rank from leader to follower, with all the associated social implications such as employee turnover, massive layoffs, share price falling, and so on.

Having been 'up close and personally digital' in a big way, enabled me to discern what causes companies to either disappear, or, ideally, to flourish and even leap frog ahead of their competitors. This resource should provide solutions characteristic to successful companies, which have accelerated their transformation and continue to keep them competitive.

DIGITAL WINDOW OF OPPORTUNITY

The IoT is at its inflection point. The window of opportunity to take advantage of the digital revolution is rapidly closing.

The Internet of Things will disrupt all businesses, including the leaders, and you can take full advantage of this transformation to your enormous benefit. Do you want your company to be a future case study for failure? The choice is entirely yours to make.

The IoT is already transforming numerous markets and companies. Making sense of these changes and more importantly, understanding how to leverage them to grow head and shoulders above your competition is one of the objectives of this book.

The IoT will connect everyone and everything into a seamless network, which Jeremy Rifkin calls the "Intelligent Third Industrial Revolution infrastructure—the Internet of Things." IoT will "usher in a fundamental reordering of human relationships, from hierarchical to lateral power, that will impact the way we conduct business, govern society, educate our children, and engage in civic life (1)".

On the opening day of the World Economic Forum in Davos, in 2015, John Chambers, Executive chairman of Cisco Systems, speaking at a session entitled "The New Digital Context", stated, "I've seen this movie before. Today we are at an inflection point. Take what happened with the Internet in the 1990s, multiply it by five to ten-fold and that's what you're about to see and the benefits are going to be seen by every single person. In short what you're going to see is every company, every country, every citizen, every home, every car, every wearable will become digitally connected. That information flow is going to allow you to change things (2)".

As a powerful indicator of this era, the sum of all data created in the next few years will be at least ten times more than the total of all data generated up to this point, jumping from around 4.4 zettabytes in 2013 to 44 zettabytes by 2020 (3). IoT is accelerating the digital transformation which started in the year 2000.

Technologies are evolving laser fast, but have not yet established their "rules of the game". That which happened to digital cameras in the 1990s and with the internet in the beginning of 2000 is what is happening to the IoT right now.

It is indeed an exciting and important time, because you have a unique opportunity to change and adapt the game rules to suit your needs and preferences, and in so doing, outperform your competitors.

In a non-technical way, as well, this book will help point to what is going on in the industry, helping to transform potential risks into opportunities. There is a new paradigm that is building up which will transform our economic, social, and political world. It's going to happen whether we like it or not. If your company is not already planning to take part in this new world, you might be losing the opportunity to lead the pack in your marketplace.

IoT WILL ~~DISRUPT~~ INDIVIDUALS

The number of IoT endpoint devices such as cars, refrigerators and everything in between will grow from **10.3** billion in 2014 to more than **29.5** billion in 2020.

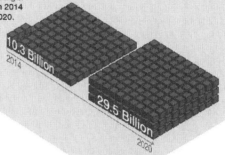

10.3 Billion
2014

29.5 Billion
2020

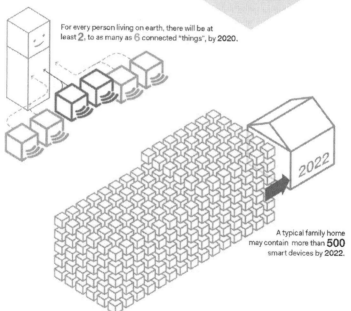

For every person living on earth, there will be at least **2**, to as many as **6** connected "things", by **2020**.

2022

A typical family home may contain more than **500** smart devices by 2022.

DIGITAL DENIAL

Are your peers saying things like this?

- We are too big to fail
- We have plenty of time
- We don't need anyone
- This is just a passing fad
- We have been doing it this way for fifteen years
- We know our market, our customers, and our channels
- These technology trends don't apply to our products
- We have already tried this and it does not work

I hear these and similar statements throughout the industry, which are all attempts to convince and appease naïve members that digital transformation trends such as the Internet of Things do not apply do their businesses. They prefer to believe that IoT is merely a buzz word or the newest fad.

If you think your company, your employees, your peers, your channels and yourself are not at risk; if you believe that you are the exception and do not need to concern yourself with digital transformation and the implications of the IoT, please do not read this book.

On the other hand, if you understand that IoT holds critical and unprecedented opportunities and risks, then this book is for you.

DISECTING THE DIGITIZATION PHENOMENON

This book will help you and your staff understand:

- why digitization is the right choice,
- why the IoT is the best bet when a company is willing to go digital and gain financial performance,
- the opportunities and risks of the IoT digital transformation,
- and finally, how to leverage digital transformation to beat commoditization and leapfrog your competition.

Some of today's analog players might be tomorrow's unicorns if they succeed with their digital transformation. The word "analog" describes companies that have not gone through a digital transformation. In market places typically dominated by analog company-derived products and services, the rules are not only changing, but in many cases, entirely new games with radically different playing fields are evolving. Industries and markets that didn't exist just a few short years ago, are sprouting up everywhere. The information within this volume is based on case studies and will explain, both simply and practically, what digital transformation means and what is the foundation of the Internet of Things.

"As we head into 2016, the IoT has gained mainstream awareness, yet organizations are still struggling with how to deal with the complexities of the vendor ecosystem in terms of developing and deploying connected products and services," says Carrie MacGillivray, Vice President responsible for IDC's Mobility and Internet of Things teams (4).

Our mission is to help companies successfully transform themselves digitally by providing a simple methodology with pragmatic steps. Such a well-defined and executed plan helps fulfill a company's social responsibility towards their employees and customers by improving their financial performance.

IoT WILL ~~DISRUPT~~ ENTREPRISES

Internet of Things, or the IoT, is an industry-specific buzzword: **87%** of people actually have no idea of what it means or what it stands for.

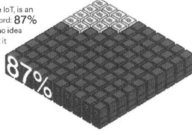

60% of those enterprises with 1,000 + employees use or plan to use IoT-enabled applications

58% of organizations throughout the world understand that IoT is strategic to their business

According to IDC, IoT will disrupt up to **33%** of the currently leading businesses

DIGITIZE TO 'PROFITIZE'

Are you aware that digital transformation and profitability are tightly linked? Companies that combine both investments in technology-enabled initiatives and associated leadership capabilities outperform their peers. They statistically derive more revenue (+9%), more profit (+26%) and have an overall higher market value (+12%) (5).

If tackled properly, digital transformation with the IoT is an enabler for financial performance. On the other hand, the opportunity becomes a significant risk if the impact and consequences are not properly understood and addressed.

SPECIFIC AUDIENCE AND UNIQUE INTENT

This book is written for the CEOs, CDOs and employees of companies that have built a performing analog business and that are asking questions about what the IoT holds in store, good or bad, for their business.

This book is intended to be used by senior leaders in manufacturing companies, resellers, software vendors and associated channels, in particular—CDOs, CTOs, and CIO/CDIOs, who are at the forefront of leading the digital transformation of the company.

We address both the threats and the opportunities presented by the Internet of Things. We balance actual company cases and market studies to form a strategy that gives companies the tools and methods needed to adapt and thrive through their digital transformation journey.

We address how the IoT will impact current analog companies, what strategies are applicable to transform a risk into an opportunity and how to focus on specific areas of IoT implications:

IoT strategies for analog companies

For analog companies that have fine-tuned their strategy throughout the years (organizations, financials flows, people, products, channels, etc.) it is vital that they keep their everyday operations (what we call the "analog mothership") working in the markets where they make their money. They need to prepare themselves for what might happen and understand the different options available when facing digital transformation.

This book focuses on what options exist to make that transformation possible in the most efficient way. It may not be necessary to change the mothership, or it may in fact need to be completely rebuilt from the ground up.

IoT technologies

IoT technologies and stabilization of the standardization landscape will have a dramatic impact on current manufacturing leaders and analog players, including software vendors and associated channels. The current IoT is far from being standardized, which brings challenges regarding cost for product development, compatibility and interoperability between products, services, and systems for manufacturers.

IoT is already changing the pace at which products and software are being brought to the market. The need for ecosystems and common reference architectures will introduce new markets such as IoT platforms and interoperability/compatibility validation organizations. The IoT will also bring major challenges around security, data ownership and related knowledge.

This book addresses the technology and innovation side of the IoT without being a technical reference manual.

IoT business models shifts

The business models and approaches which take advantage of the Internet of Things require an understanding of the implications and opportunities presented. Traditional business models have been well-suited for processes, people, products and everything else for a specific analog market. However, the rules are changing and those changes are accelerating rapidly.

This book addresses the different model shifts implied by the IoT on both capex (capital expenditures) and Opex (operating expenses) perspectives, such as product-to-product system data, product to services, and products as a service.

The importance of channels, ecosystems, and strategy execution
The rules of the game might change in the marketplaces typically dominated by your company's products and services. There are many options available as you work your way through the planning process. For example, are your products still marketable in the new paradigm? You may feel these products define your corporate identity, which may make it difficult to conceive of some of the changes you need to confront.

This book focuses on the importance of channels and ecosystems that might evolve and impact your operations.

The importance of people and organizations
The biggest challenge of the transition to the IoT lies in the human factor. A company is, among all hard and soft assets, made up primarily of a group of people. In fact, the most valuable corporate assets are often the people they employ.

Middle management plays a pivotal role when dealing with digital transformation.

Analog company leaders willing to embrace the IoT should help the company's middle management to understand the goals and outcomes, as well as the risks and threats to the existing business.

Setting a vision and giving a purpose to the mission is not only about defining what needs to be done. It is ultimately about creating the environment in which employees can challenge the status quo, creating enhancements to the business model, processes, products, and services, as well as the corporation itself.

For managers in traditional industries, this can be a tall order. Many current CTOs come from a "good old analog" industry and must discover and learn about the digital side of the coin instead of focusing only on their R&D. Applying yesterday's successful recipe will no longer work.

Many assumptions about what is possible and impossible, based on experience with last century's technologies, are no longer valid in the digital world. How do you move beyond your current mindset to find opportunities that digital technology can support and enable?

The challenge is how to make those people understand the new realities and how to bring solutions to them. They have tremendous experience and understand the marketplace, so it is vital to include transitioning the existing workforce as part of your strategy.

This book focuses on the importance of the 'why'. The challenge resides in the digital transformation of middle management.

FINDING CERTAINTY IN UNCERTAIN TIMES: A UNIQUE METHOD WITH A STEP BY STEP PATH TO DIGITIZATION

Choosing the best and most comprehensive possible strategy is difficult. Finding one that works for your circumstances, staff and marketplace, which also considers everything that IoT brings to the table, including channels, portfolios, and technologies, is the challenge.

The methodology proposed in this book, known as **IoT^4**, is designed to be a concise methodology to guide you through four simple digitization steps. It provides a framework for understanding your company's unique digital situation and working out a solution to maximize the transformation of your current analog portfolio and avoid commoditization.

WHAT THIS RESOURCE IS NOT

You should not read this book if you are looking for a list of all existing IoT norms, standards, technologies and applications (often called "Smart Something").

This book is not a technical volume as there are plenty of white papers, case studies, and books available that go over this technology in detail. Instead, this book will define some terms and processes without going into detail; just enough technology will be described to ensure understanding.

This book is not a discussion about which technologies are likely to win or lose. Predictions about which companies will likely make it versus those that may fail are beyond the scope of this manuscript.

We do not believe in focusing on "Smart Something" (Smart Energy, Smart Industry, etc.) as the industry has already moved beyond this concept and it does not respond to the challenges which companies need to face in taking advantage of digital technology.

Instead, we will give you all the necessary knowledge to understand what is happening and, more importantly, what options you and your business must leverage this major milestone in digital transformation.

CHAPTER 1

DEFINITIONS AND DYNAMICS FOR ANALOG LEADERS

*"Expect the unexpected. And whenever possible, be the unexpected.
Jack Dorsey, creator and co-founder of Twitter"*

DIGITAL TRANSFORMATION JITTERS

Are you having doubts and concerns about what the IoT has in store for your business? Do you have questions about the possible strategic options available for your company to leverage in the IoT?

Are you concerned about well-financed, young companies that will become tomorrow's 'unicorns' and are encroaching on your traditional sales channels and marketplaces? The word 'unicorn' in this industry was first defined by the venture capitalist Aileen Lee, founder of CowboyVC, as "U.S.-based software companies started after 2003 and valued at over $1 billion by public or private market investors (6)".

Do you wonder and ask yourself what your CEO (Chief Executive Officer), Chief Digital Officer (CDO), Chief Technology Officer (CTO) and Chief Digital Information Officer (CDIO/CIO) and associated middle management can do to take advantage of IoT to transform your company? Would you like to avoid failures like those of Nokia and Kodak to digitally transform, which led to their loss of significant market share (7)?

You may have doubts and you may be very concerned about what the future has in store for your business, stockholders, team members and even you personally.

There is a concern about the consequences of digital transformation. These questions are vital not only for a company's survival but for its prosperity and growth.

ANALOG CAVEATS ARE ITS ULTIMATE ADVANTAGE

The word "analog" describes companies that have not gone through a digital transformation. In market places typically dominated by analog company-derived products and services, the rules are not only changing, but in many cases, entirely new games with radically different playing fields are evolving. Industries and markets that didn't exist just a few short years ago, are sprouting up everywhere.

There are thousands of young companies creating new products, services, business models and ecosystems which have already begun to revolutionize the world. In the coming years, these companies and others to follow will encroach on the more traditional markets and if nothing is done, any company, no matter how large, might be negatively impacted and shareholders will likely see their stock values reduced.

Nevertheless, analog companies have weapons at their disposal to fight back and even lead the digital transformation. It's not too late for incumbents/analog companies to adapt, especially if they leverage their considerable assets and resources to counteract the attacks (8).

These assets (8) include:

- Investment capital
- Production capabilities
- Strong brands
- Strong channels
- In-depth relationships with global accounts
- Mobilization of Sales force on the ground
- Influence power: standardization, market price, specifiers, etc.

Perhaps you feel that you have your analog business sewn up tightly enough that you don't need to worry about any of the changes that are happening. Or you might not see significant opportunities in adopting or incorporating these new technologies into your strategies. Possibly, you even believe that your products don't fit this new market, or that you have plenty of time to consider your options carefully—and that in short, you can gradually and even slowly move into this brave new world.

Unfortunately, in the meantime, your competitors may have already defined digital transformation strategies and even be in the process of implementing solutions that could jeopardize your business and traditional market share. In a worst-case scenario, they could even drive you completely out of your marketplace.

HOW TO ASSESS IF YOUR COMPANY IS DIGITAL OR IF THE MARKET PLACE IS SHIFTING

As previously stated in the introduction, a good way to assess if your company is digital or analog is to listen to the employees. If you are hearing statements on why digitization is not a concern, such as:

- We are too big to fail
- We have plenty of time
- We don't need anyone
- This is just a passing fad
- We have been doing it this way for fifteen years
- We know our market, our customers, and our channels
- These technology trends don't apply to our products

Then yes: you are in an analog company.

A way to assess if your market place is shifting to digital, is to look out of the trends on:

- Customer usages and expectations; have the customers' expectations recently shifted for more customization, more personal experience with your products, for a more intimate relationship between users and technology providers?
- Technology acceleration: Are you seeing an acceleration into customization of the usage of the hardware and software with an increase need to reduce the time lap between the rise of a new function by users and the delivery of such a function?
- Commoditization, Standardization and Globalization: is your market place getting "standardized" with consortiums or associations of companies pushing for global technology standards? Very often this is an important indicator that the once well protected analog market is getting commoditized and that it will get digitized to sustain differentiation.

IoT IS A GROWTH AREA

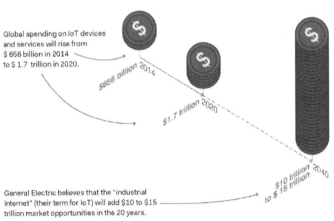

Global spending on IoT devices and services will rise from $ 656 billion in 2014 to $ 1.7 trillion in 2020.

$656 billion 2014

$1.7 trillion 2020

$10 trillion 2040 to $ 15 trillion

General Electric believes that the "industrial Internet" (their term for IoT) will add $10 to $15 trillion market opportunities in the 20 years.

IN 2025

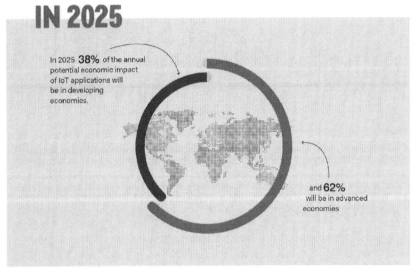

In 2025 **38%** of the annual potential economic impact of IoT applications will be in developing economies.

and **62%** will be in advanced economies

DEFINING IoT & ITS MARKETS

Before discussing various IoT strategies, we need to clarify some terms and acronyms:

- The *Internet of Things*, known as IoT, has been defined in Recommendation ITU-T Y.2060 (06/2012) as "a global infrastructure for the information society, enabling advanced services by interconnecting (physical and virtual) things based on existing and evolving interoperable information and communication technologies (9)". The Internet of Things (IoT) is often also called machine-to-machine, machine-to-infrastructure, machine-to-environment, the Internet of Everything, the Internet of Intelligent Things and Smart "something."

- *Machine-to-machine*, known as M2M, refers to the technologies that enable devices which exist on a network to exchange information and perform their prerequisite tasks without needing guidance or help from people. European Telecommunications Standards Institute defines it as follows: "M2M Communications: refer to physical telecommunication based interconnection for data exchange between two ETSI M2M compliant entities, like: device, gateways and network infrastructure (10)".

- The *Industrial Internet of Things,* known as IIoT, refers to using the Internet of Things in the manufacturing process. National Instruments gives a good in-depth definition: "The IIoT can be characterized as a vast number of connected industrial systems that are communicating and coordinating their data analytics and actions to improve industrial performance and benefit society as a whole. Industrial systems that interface the digital world to the physical world through sensors and actuators that solve complex control problems are commonly known as cyber-physical systems. These systems are being combined with Big Analog Data

solutions to gain deeper insight through data and analytics (11)".
IIoT is a subset of the IoT.

IoT = M2M rebranded and renewed

It is commonly believed that IoT is a new technology that is part of a new world of science fiction, or that it's still far off in the undefined future. In fact, IoT is a buzzword that describes the rebranding of the existing machine-to-machine (M2M) market currently in existence in a more open, consistent ecosystem and global landscape of actors (manufacturers, software providers, system integrators, developers, etc.).

Current M2M manufacturers have been selling programmable logic controllers (PLCs) and distributed control systems (DCS) since the 1990s. They then connected them into systems: and have been doing so for the last fifteen years. Although these M2M verticalized applications and systems were based on industry-standard protocols and architectures, they are not only challenging to design but also to maintain at a reasonable cost. IoT will enable horizontal system architectures, creating new rules around products such as: reliability, robustness, cost, simplicity of usage, features sets, maintenance, integration capabilities and more, while at the same time addressing and solving vertical system architectures such as performance, availability and traceability in a more open and cost-effective way.

DIGITAL TRANSFORMATION

Our manufacturing world and its ecosystem of partners, developers and customers is undergoing a paradigm evolution. It's a profound change which is already affecting markets once considered protected from any revolutionary technology shifts, such as housing and traveling. Airbnb, and Uber take over these industries as the super-unicorns and car manufacturers such as Renault, Volkswagen, and Ford are getting attacked by Tesla, Google cars and so forth.

The IoT will connect not only things with things, people with things and people with people, but it will unleash an unprecedented flow of data. Owning the source of data, building value from it and improving the business relevancy of your offers to the end user will be amongst the game changers. The game will be less about selling products than owning the relationship and the data. Tomorrow's winners will be the ones that have managed to not only connect their customers, but have made sense of the consequential flow of data to the end user.

Digital transformation has been happening for more than twenty years; the IoT is one of many milestones of digitization in our society and economy, but it is unique in that it will release an amount of data and information, previously inaccessible. This will then create the conditions to allow the next digital transformation, which will include virtual reality, analytics, artificial intelligence and deep knowledge.

In the coming years, some businesses will be able to adjust, change, and thrive in this new era. Others will battle to survive but will come out better from it in the end. Still more, perhaps the majority, will not recognize the change or will be unable to adjust. Within a few years, they might be struggling to survive after competitors will have managed to leverage these transformations to their benefit and consequently, overtake and commoditize their markets.

During his interview with Box CEO Aaron Levie, John Chambers, executive chairman of Cisco Systems, got the keynote audience's attention at the BoxWorks 2015 conference (box.com) when he said, "At least 40 percent of all businesses will die in the next 10 years... if they don't figure out how to change their entire company to accommodate new technologies (12)".

The potential consequences of these transformations on consumers and businesses are important. Entire industries are changing before our very eyes and the way companies do business is already altering and will be vastly different in just a few years.

The question for you is, does IoT change the way you have been doing business?

IoT will consist of billions, and in the relatively near future potentially trillions, of smart, interconnected devices called "things," all communicating through the Internet in a kind of global neural network. These smart machines will interact and confer with people, the environment, other machines, infrastructures and each other to accomplish tasks and provide services hitherto unimaginable.

IoT is not a revolution as such, but just another step in the digital transformation journey of our society. The big change of the IoT is the fact that it unleashes data that was previously out of range (due to legacy protocols, non-connected products, etc.). This opens the door to new services, new integrations and new business models while at the same time challenging the existing go-to-markets, ecosystems, alliances, proactive and curative maintenance offers, services and operations of today's analog manufacturers.

There is no doubt that IoT will change the lives of everyone, from the consumer all the way up to manufacturers and large corporations. Just as Uber and Airbnb have changed the world of transportation and lodging, other forms of transformation will affect individual routines such as working, purchasing, traveling, communicating and being entertained.

The old analog business models may no longer be adapted to these transformations. Companies, such as Polaroid, that in the recent past faced similar market evolution to digitization were unable to adapt their operating procedures or to transition quickly enough to take advantage of the new technologies, have faced grave difficulties.

The underlying question you should be asking is how and where you will be able to take advantage of these technologies to grow your company, lest your business declines and fades away.

Will you be able to use your existing staff and infrastructure to leverage these new opportunities? Can you move out of your comfort zone and handle the unique and changing challenges of these new paradigms?

It is important for you to understand that this is far more than just a change in the rules that you've been playing within your analog business for years and even decades. The old games are becoming obsolete and will be replaced by entirely new rules, playing fields, playing pieces, and referees.

In the future, the rate of adoption for new technologies will be measured in months, weeks, or even days. The IoT is not a technology game changer; rather, it enables us to enter a world of:

- Data bulimia (an unmanageable amount of data)
- Connectivity between things and things, but also between people and things
- Digital in-security
- Pay as you need

If you're not convinced, have a look at how digital transformation has been impacting companies in different ways. These changes will affect all industries, some more quickly than others:

- Telecommunications: In the past, it took more than seventy years for telephones to be adopted in 50 percent of the households in the United States; radio required only twenty-five years, and Internet access less than ten. More recently, Facebook took 852 days to reach ten million users, Twitter required 780 days and Google Plus only needed sixteen days (13).

- Banking: BBVA CEO and chairman Francisco Gonzalez has a stark warning: "Up to half of the world's banks will disappear through the cracks opened up by digital disruption of the industry (14)".
- Companies such as Google, Facebook and Amazon, among others, are threatening the banking industry. Gonzales believes that technological change continues apace and society is changing with it. "We are witnessing the dawn of Big Data technology; the Internet of Things is just taking off and Artificial Intelligence is in its infancy. So, we are running a race which has no finish line, nor a pre-fixed route. We don't even have a set of rules to guide us in our efforts (15)" González concluded in the Strategy Research Conference, organized by the Harvard Business School to analyze how large multinationals are changing their strategies to respond to technological change.
- Phones: Microsoft acquired Nokia in late 2013 (16) to popularize the Windows 10 platform on smartphones. Unfortunately, their efforts were too little too late, as the immensely popular Android and iOS platforms already had the market sewn up tight. Thus, even though the Windows 10 operating system is very well regarded (17), consumers were reluctant to make the jump to the new phone without applications and developers were reluctant to write applications without consumers.

DIGITAL MATURITY LEADS TO INCREASED FINANCIAL PERFORMANCE

In 2002, Capgemini Consulting published their online report, 'How Digital Leaders Outperform their Peers in Every Industry' after performing surveys on 391 companies and analyzing 184 publicly traded companies to assess their digital maturity. Importantly, the results were linked to their industry-adjusted financial performance (5).

According to Capgemini, digital maturity means to invest in technology enabled initiatives while at the same time, enabling digital transformation leadership.

They separated those two dimensions into four different categories and found that the companies that combine investments both in technology-enabled initiatives as well as the leadership capabilities outperform their peers. They statistically derive more revenue from their physical assets (+9%), are more profitable (+26%) and have overall higher market valuations (+12%).

Another study, The Path to Digital Transformation (18), shows that digital transformation has the following positive impacts:

- Four years are needed before there are financial results from the digital transformation.
- The average net promotor score by customers will be 86% on average.
- 55% of employees, on average, will have knowledge of digital capabilities.
- On average, 45% of products will be ordered online.

Digitization might have different faces and might be understood differently when talking about technologies, organizations, channels and so forth. However, it is without doubt a major contributor to financial performance, customer satisfaction and market valuation.

DIGITAL
TRANSFORMATION

**BENEFITS TO COMPANIES INVESTING IN BOTH IN TECHNOLOGY-ENABLED
INITIATIVES AND LEADERSHIP CAPABILITIES**

Generate more
revenue

+9%

Are more
profitable

+26%

Have an overall
higher market
value

+12%

BIGGEST DIGITAL THREATS: INTERNAL OR EXTERNAL

Internal Issues : Lack of agility, complacency,
inflexible culture **19%**

Market Disruptions : Product obsolescence, lower
barriers to entry **17%**

Competitive Pressure : More intense competition,
faster or new competitors **16%**

Security issues : **14%**

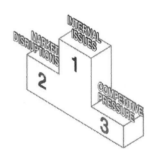

24% of organizations throughout
the world recognize that IoT will
transform their business

25% of companies surveyed
are willing to disrupt themselves
in order to compete

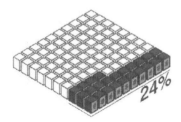

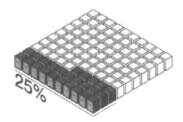

DIGITIZATION: TREPIDATION ABOUT WHAT IS COMING

A survey done by Gartner in July 2016 (19), showed that 91 percent of the surveyed IT professionals had doubts about their roles in their organization's digital transformation. However, 59 percent added that their IT organization were unprepared for the digital business of the next two years.

You can choose to ignore the opportunities, but you will not be able to sidestep the repercussions of the IoT.

As of today, there are opportunities for both existing and new players. Digitization enables technology companies to compete with historical analog businesses (20). Leading tire manufacturers such as Michelin, for example, are creating new business models to leverage the IoT to accelerate their transformation, leapfrogging Chinese commoditization manufacturers by moving from product-based business to a disruptive service-based business model (21) .

Looking at the past and at similar digital transformation is a good way to understand what might happen. An example is the story of Nokia.

Are you aware of what happened to this company?

Before 2007, Nokia practically owned the world of smartphones on the global market. Today, their market share has declined and continues to give up ground to competition from the iPhone and Android products (22). Nokia was so large that this drop would have been unthinkable at the time, yet they have not managed to evolve. Now they are desperately playing catch-up.

In 2007, Nokia controlled approximatively 40 percent of the market. By the end of 2015, Nokia's market share sat at 15 percent, thanks to a horde of cheaper basic phones, according to data compiled by Strategy Analytics (23). In fact, by the end of 2016, Nokia has largely vanished from the smartphone market (22).

Mobile phone numbers will rise from just over 7 billion in 2015 to 8.6 billion by 2021, with connected device numbers passing those for mobile phones in 2018 (24). During the same period, the number of IoT devices (connected cars, machines, utility meters, etc.) will more than triple between 2015 and 2021 (24).

Don't be misled by the self-declared technology gurus that the digital revolution is simply yet another evolution of technology. The Internet of Things is an industry-specific buzzword and almost 90% of the population have no idea what it means (25).

DIGITAL CASE IN POINT: KODAK

Ignoring or minimizing the impact that IoT could have on your business might result in a shrinking market share, a smaller customer base and falling profit margins. The risks associated with doing nothing or moving too slowly could be as significant as the loss of the company itself.

To illustrate, consider the sometimes-forgotten case of digital transformation, Kodak:

Many people don't remember that Kodak was the undisputed king of photography for much of the late twentieth century. Given the fact that Kodak's core business was selling film, it's not very difficult to understand how the last twenty years have been challenging to the well-established analog leader, with the fast and furious advent of digital cameras, smartphones and cloud technologies. Today the company has a market capitalization of roughly $635 million (26), which plummeted from $30 billion in the 1990s due to competition from digital photography (27).

Simply put, Kodak failed to embrace the new technology. CEO George Fisher told the *New York Times* that Kodak had "regarded digital photography as the enemy, an evil juggernaut that would kill the chemical-based film and paper business that fueled Kodak's sales and profits for decades (28)". Their failure was the result of their inability to truly embrace the new business models of disruptive change. Kodak failed at realizing "that online photo sharing was the new business, not just a way to expand the printing business (29)".

The company filed for bankruptcy protection in 2012, exited its legacy analog businesses and sold off its patents. The fact that Kodak practically invented the digital camera and owned the patents on that technology makes this even more ironic.

The risks associated with doing nothing or moving too slowly could also impact the ability of your company to seek new financing which would allow for a strong come back or to catch up with other players that have better managed to pivot and re-think their operations, their people and the way they do business.

You might believe the IoT is growing slowly, giving you plenty of time to strategize and transition your business to this new paradigm. However, the number of things—smart devices of all types—connected to the Internet is growing exponentially. Gartner predicts that the number connected will increase from 6.4 billion in 2016 to 20.8 billion by 2020 (30).

Unfortunately, time is a scarce resource, even more so when technologies, market and competition acceleration reduce the time left to react and adapt to the new rules of the game.

EVOLUTION OF BUSINESS MODELS

"Smart" connected devices promise to improve the quality of life in the consumer world and to reduce costs and increase efficiencies for businesses.

Vertical business models, which postulate specialized devices targeted for specific environments, promise to change the way whole segments of the economy operate. For example, one would think that an elevator has nothing to do with high tech and IoT technologies. Connecting elevators and their components by itself brings no value, but unleashing the data that was inaccessible before opens new opportunities, new services, new business models and more. Connecting elevators could enable companies like Schindler Group, Kone, and Otis Elevator to have a more predictive approach on maintenance and therefore reduce unavailability time and raise end user satisfaction while at the same time increase their profitability by reducing curative maintenance interventions.

Horizontal business models, at the same time, strive to allow multiple vendors to use a common standardized technology stack. This allows these vendors to take advantage of cloud-based standards and equipment to simplify communications and control. This integrates devices of all kinds into a common structure, making it easier for users to operate and allowing manufacturers to focus on designing devices, software and services.

For example, tomorrow's houses will be the nest of such horizontal business models, connecting all sorts of devices in a manner reminiscent of Lego™ bricks, enabling infinite variations and combinations to be created to suit your specific needs. IoT will create the conditions that enable customization and personalization of your environment. Additionally, massive amounts of data about you, your environment and your rituals will be created, stored and analyzed. IoT will create the conditions that will see artificial intelligence relying on big data analytics becoming the next digital transformation.

If you are an analog company, you must get ready to take advantage of these evolutions and assess if those digital transformations will impact your business in one way or another. To begin the process, you need to understand why IoT is a unique opportunity to accelerate and leapfrog your competitors.

THE IMPORTANCE OF STRATEGIC TIMING

There is a common belief that first in are always the winners; in other words, that to leverage a digital transformation innovation, the first is the one that takes it all. This belief is false.

In their book, *Pioneer Advantage: Marketing Logic or Marketing Legend?* (31) Gerard J. Tellis and Peter N. Golder analyzed approximately five hundred brands in fifty product categories. The results show that almost half of the market pioneers fail and their mean market share is much lower than that found in other studies. They state: "Our results suggest that being first in a new market may not confer automatic long-term rewards. An alternative strategy worth considering may be to let other firms pioneer and explore markets, and enter after learning more about the structure and dynamics of the market. Indeed, early leaders who entered an average of 13 years after the pioneer are more likely than pioneers to lead markets today. The reason is that the early leaders entered decisively and committed large resources to building and leading the market. The logic of success is not to be first to enter the market, but to strive for leadership by scanning opportunities, building on strengths and committing resources to serve consumers effectively."

Looking at the Kodak case from the perspective of Gerard J. Tellis and Peter N. Golder's study, it is important to understand that the main root cause of Kodak's failure was a mistaken strategic framing of what the digital transformation meant for new business models, adapting resource allocation and overall timing.

Kodak had a good strategy and the means to execute it, but paid the price of wanting to be the pioneers and not setting the right model in place. The underlying subject around people, leadership, and middle management should not be underestimated when addressing digital transformation (this also applies to Kodak).

In the next chapter, we will be looking at the people and organization aspect of the IoT digital transformation.

CHAPTER 2

WHAT IS CHANGING?
WHAT CAN YOU DO ABOUT IT?

"In the new world, it is not the big fish which eats the small fish, it's the fast fish which eats the slow fish (32)"
Klaus Schwab, founder and executive chairman, World Economic Forum

LOOKING BACK: FROM MAINFRAMES TO IOT

To understand where IoT comes from, we need to look back at least fifty years. In the history of the Internet and computing, there were three distinct and overlapping periods that resulted in a shift towards three types of businesses:

- In the first period (1950–1980), companies used large mainframes with centralized computer centers and application software. These machines took up entire air-conditioned rooms and provided the most basic of computing resources. One of these machines alone—many company computer rooms had several—could cost upwards of a million dollars, and sometimes hundreds of thousands of dollars per year in addition to maintain. Processing was batched and the results of the computations often were not available for hours or even days. Each of these computers served many people, sometimes whole departments or even whole companies. Employees who wanted to leverage the computing power of those mainframes had to bring their work to those centers and the data was input to the machines via magnetic tape, punch cards and even paper tape.
- In the second period (1980–2000), companies such as Cisco and 3com built the backbone of the Internet by installing routers, switches and other networking equipment. During this time, these and other suppliers of the equipment built up the network so it became the dominant force in the marketplace. This period is all about PC-enabled systems and networks with software distributed in both servers and client computers. The first desktop computers began appearing. These were relatively large boxes which sat on top of or beside a desk. Each person had one computer and processing took anywhere from minutes to hours. These desktop computing systems generally cost from $1,000 to $3,000. However, this was a vast improvement over the computing resources available just a decade before. Employees

had enough computing power on their computer to handle work from their location.

- In the third period (2000–today), companies such as Google and Yahoo provide services that include search, email, and so forth. These companies grew much more quickly than those in the first period and came to dominate their marketplace. Now that the infrastructures and tools were in place, large businesses such as Amazon could take hold and grow. The expansion of these companies and their digital revolution occurred even faster, in a matter of a few years. Smaller desktop units and laptops became more and more common. These were more mobile and required access to a network to perform useful work. They were very fast, especially in comparison to older computers and returned results in seconds or a few minutes. Generally, each person uses one of these computers on their desk at their office and they also have one in their home. This period is all about the Internet, virtualized computers and global network enablement. Software is decoupled from the hardware. Employees can now work from anywhere and have access to nearly all connected information and connected computing power to handle their work.

Interestingly, if you look at the length of the waves—thirty, twenty, and sixteen years—the speed of innovation and the associated digital transformation of our society seems to be accelerating. Very often the length of a digital and innovation wave (from first users to deployment everywhere) is more or less the lifetime of the equipment.

Machine-2-machine began in the second period and relied on the connectivity provided by the network. This took off in the third wave, which has enabled huge transformations.

Robotics, for example, has directly benefited from the M2M digital transformation:

- 2000–2010: The Open Source Robotics Foundation developed an open source robotic operating system (33) that enabled various robotic technologies to be developed and tested. In 2004, DARPA (Defense Advanced Research Project Agency) funded a competition to develop autonomous military vehicles, which allowed automobile manufacturers to become involved with military and civilian autonomous systems (34).
- 2010 onward: As technology improves, robots are getting better at decision-making and becoming more autonomous. Machines are even beginning to possess visual perception and speech recognition and are automating tasks that previously could only be performed by humans. In fact, DARPA and the military are funding projects to create autonomous drones for use in the air, in the sea and on the land.

But why is IoT going to accelerate what we have been experiencing for the last fifteen years?

WHAT IS CHANGING?

Freeing up data that was previously (and is still) inaccessible and enabling more intelligence in and outside the products and environment that surrounds us is, in fact, the real enabler and the first step to the next digital milestone.

Unleashing data will enable the connection of everyone and everything in a seamless network and the creation of knowledge and value around this uninterrupted flow of data. This will have increasingly dramatic effects on the lives of everyone on the planet.

Over the next decade, the IoT and related technologies will free human beings from doing routine and mundane tasks. This will enable them to focus on activities that are more fulfilling and involve more creativity.

Big data will be moving from an analog model to digital, which will require manufacturers to quickly change their business structure and channels to adapt. Analytics will then transform big data into knowledge, allowing more understanding and control and then into intelligence.

The promise of IoT is immense—not as a technology, but in how it unleashes data and what it enables, such as:

- Connected products
- Connected services (preventive and corrective maintenance, for example)
- Connected customers
- Augmented reality
- Virtual reality
- Predictive analytics
- Artificial intelligence and deep learning

SO WHAT IS CHANGING?

ESTIMATES OF CONNECTED DEVICES IN 2020 (in billions)

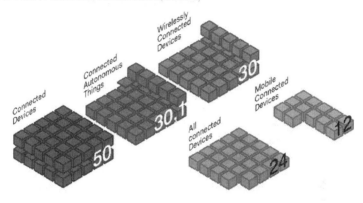

IOT MARKET DRIVERS AND BARRIERS

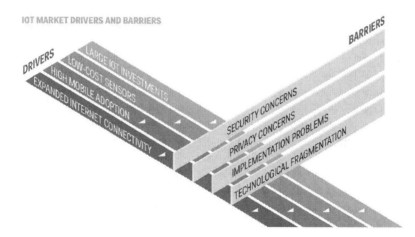

If you take a step back, all those promises stem mainly from changes such as:

Technologies

Most individuals and businesses are concerned about technology and wonder how it will affect them. IoT is a technical subject with many acronyms, architectures, and so on, which can be very intimidating and confusing. We will address the technical aspects of the IoT in Chapter 5 of this book for you to understand the underlying technologies, standards and how innovation plays an important role.

Ecosystems (hardware, software providers, community of developers, etc.)

If you have been manufacturing or selling "analog" cars for thirty years, you will certainly understand that manufacturing and selling a digitally connected product requires the evolution of your ecosystem of partners, such that your go-to-market product will possibly vary accordingly. For example, the focus in connected cars is shifting from the dashboard to vehicle data. Look at what is happening to this market in the last couple of years; you have plenty of newcomers such as Apple CarPlay, Androidauto, Carvoyant, Dash, and Vinli.

Even the analog manufacturers recognize that ecosystems will be playing a huge role in the digitization of the analog industry: According to Don Butler, Executive director of connected vehicles and services at Ford, access to vehicle data needs to be controlled (35). Steffen Neumann, Application Portfolio Manager at Mercedes-Benz, also highlights the importance of controlling the HMI, UI and the whole safety aspect (35). As stated in "IoT Megatrends 2016", "Developers are a driving force in every IoT industry and a source of competitive advantage. Every IoT company should master the human art of managing developer ecosystems (36)". This is described in Chapter 8.

Channels (system integrators, distributors, wholesalers, etc.)

Many businesses are beginning to understand that digital channels are becoming important, and that to succeed in the future they must transition over to these new paradigms. As an example, the collision of both OT (Operational Technologies) and IT (Information Technologies) channels/partners/system integrators in building management will be evolving in the coming years into a more collaborative environment and ecosystem between all players of the value chain to deliver the expected integration that the IoT promises. We will also see the evolution of those players from Capex-driven to Opex-driven business models, leveraging analytics and off-site services such as predictive maintenance. This is described in Chapter 7.

Business models

To survive the changes that are coming, businesses, no matter how small or large, must innovate and work to disrupt their own business models. They must work quickly to design and implement strategies to reposition their organizations, retrain their staff (or hire new people), and refocus their efforts.

The business model in IoT is moving from one-off sales to recurrent revenue. But don't be misled by this; there is still a huge product market out there, but the rules of the game will be very different than those of today. As stated by Cap Gemini, "There is no neat one-size-fits-all monetization model for the IoT, not least because the needs of different companies vary hugely (37)" and "Product selling is an organization's entry into the IoT world (38)". Choosing the best possible business model adapted to your current portfolio and strategy is very often where offer managers struggle.

Another aspect of the shift in business models is that consumer and enterprise technologies are increasingly converging in many industries.

Unfortunately, few of these businesses and their management realize how quickly they must change and how significant those changes need to be.

If you take General Electric as an example, what they have accomplished in recent years is quite impressive. Jeff Immelt is changing GE's positioning and its associate portfolio; divesting 60 percent of the company he took over in 2001 while developing at the same time its IIoT-based solutions and partnering with Cisco and PTC to carry out its mission (39). According to Bill Ruh, CEO of GE Digital and CDO for GE, "If software experts truly knew what Jeff Immelt and GE Digital were doing, there's no other software company on the planet where they would rather be (40)". This is described further in Chapter 7.

People:
As will be described in Chapter 8, businesses no longer have the luxury of ample time to make this transition into the new paradigm of the Internet of Things. There are young, upstart companies working diligently to come up with new products, services and delivery methods which will make the way you do business obsolete sooner rather than later. The IoT will have a direct impact on workforces; this includes the people that are within the analog business, plus those team members dedicated to the new digital technology, plus the staff that straddles both worlds. Middle management will be in the thick of these changes.

WHY IS DATA IMPORTANT AND WHY CONNECTING CUSTOMERS' ASSETS IS CRITICAL FOR YOUR FUTURE?
The difference between just selling hardware or using the data and connecting the customer's assets is the difference between making a single sale and receiving a recurrent, predictable flow of money. Wouldn't your business be better off making a regular income from services than just making a one-shot sale?

It is vital to connect devices to the cloud to ensure you have a recurrent flow of raw data that will then enable you to serve customers with asset management, predictive maintenance, advanced analytics, etc. Take elevators for example. An elevator goes up and down 200 times per day. Combine this with the fact that the flywheel in the elevator is two years old, added to the knowledge of when they commonly fail, allows you to send out repair men before it breaks.

THE VALUE OF INTEROPERABILITY

INTEROPERABILITY IS A CRITICAL SOURCE OF VALUE IN IOT SYSTEMS

STAND ALONE   INTEROPERABLE DEVICES

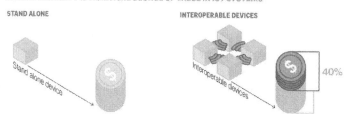

We estimate that situations in which two or more IoT systems must work together accounts for approximately 40% of the total value which can be unlocked by the Internet of Things.

According to our estimation of IoTs maximum potential, we have included the benefits of interoperability. Without these benefits, we estimate the maximum value of the applications would be only about **$7 trillion** per year in 2025, rather than **$11.1 trillion**.

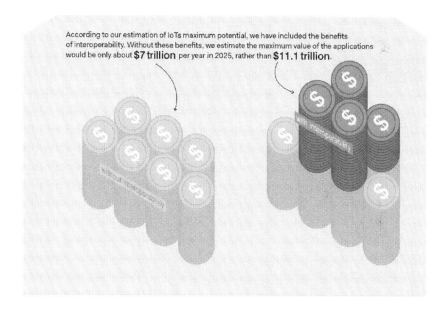

Companies that send out technicians for preventive maintenance save their customers' money and inconvenience. Replacement of parts before they break means that maintenance can be scheduled at times that are more convenient for the business and reduce downtime dramatically. In other words, you can plan for preventive maintenance. This is a service that customers will pay for on a recurrent basis.

This value is created and enhanced by the data which illustrates why it is important for manufacturers to get all their assets connected. The rawer the data you collect from your end user, the more you can build knowledge and deliver better value. This enables manufacturers and system integrators to create recurrent revenue streams.

If your products are not operating in the cloud, this may very quickly turn into a roadblock to delivering best in class services your customers expect. For example, if all you're doing is selling hardware which doesn't connect with other systems as well as the cloud, then you will have difficulties creating recurring revenue streams.

Connecting assets and leveraging the resulting flow of data to build unique advance software services such as analytics will not only drive end user satisfaction but also accelerate their overall financial performance. Not only does this bring more recurring revenue but it also enables the companies to have a more in-depth, added value relationship with their end-users and therefore be more business relevant for their operations. Being more business relevant enables companies to have a more captive installed base of customers, avoid commoditization and enhance end user satisfaction.

WHAT CAN YOU DO ABOUT IT? ANALOG PLAYERS' STRATEGIC OPTIONS

The fact is that IoT changes the rules of the game in some of these areas. And in some areas, IoT changes the game entirely. The completely new business models adopted by Airbnb and Uber illustrate how severe the disruption can be.

Manufacturers need to be not only willing and able but nimble in pivoting quickly in this fast-moving technological revolution. Changes will occur at lightning speed, both in technology and the marketplace and the consumers' tastes will probably change alongside at every blink of an eye.

When studying companies that have been faced with the need for change and disruption in the last decade, data shows that there are multiple scenarios which describe their approaches.

IoT and the potential disruptions it may cause also comply with those four scenarios:

Option #1: Ignore and/Put Off

Choosing to ignore these technologies and the digital transformation they implicate, is a convenient option. Ignoring is a deliberate choice; it will, at best, prevent your business from profiting from the changes. At worst, your analog business will find itself floundering and eventually may even fail.

Indefinitely procrastinating may be a related choice, due to trepidation, budgetary or resource limitations or plain naiveté in thinking you are too big to fail or that the new paradigm doesn't apply. The challenges will only become bigger and more complicated.

Option #2: Milk the cow

Another strategy is to milk the cow; in other words, to continue doing what you've been doing without embracing the digitization of the environment in which your company operates. The difference with option #1, is that in this option, a conscious decision is made to take advantage of your current market position without, deliberately preparing for the future.

This strategy is all about leveraging your current market position and associated organization, channels, operations and so forth, to deliver financial performance without the burden, and associated financial impacts, of going through digital transformation of your portfolio, organization and so forth.

The advantage that the newcomers have when a market begins to evolve due to digitization, is in fact also a disadvantage for them concerning the historical analog businesses and channels. Very often the cost of entering those analog marketplaces is so high, not only from a technological aspect but also when considering the channels, manufacturing and logistics capabilities, patents, etc., that it places important barriers keeping your analog a safe haven, at least for a while. Unfortunately, this analog safe haven is, sooner or later, being attacked by the digital newcomers. This is the option that Kodak chose, and it served them well for several years until the quality of the technology improved and the cost decreased. By that time, it was too late for Kodak to change direction, but they did thrive for several years leveraging their analog market place predominant position.

Option #3: U-turn the mothership

You can try to move the mothership; in other words, you can attempt to implement the new paradigm throughout your organization and marketplace. This process is extremely difficult and complicated, and the risk is very high. Changing existing procedures, markets, and processes can prove to be impossible and the likelihood of failure is high. This scenario also assumes there is time to research products and services, hire or retrain staff and restructure or reorient the business as appropriate.

Option #4: Transforming from the edge

A better option is to maintain your existing markets and channels—keep the mothership afloat—while investing money into creating a new opportunity at the edge of your core offerings. You could liken this to an organ transplant: you're keeping the body alive while you change out the other parts for newer and more modern parts.

As stated by Alan Lewis and Dan McKone's in their book *Edge Strategy: A new mindset for profitable growth* (41); Edge strategies are less risky and can bring a higher return than many other options when a company needs to grow their revenue and associated profits. The risk and the resulting costs, are often subsidized by another area of the organization, very often the historical analog part of the business, which has the capacity to carry such financial burden thanks to its healthier balance sheet.

Edge strategies are ideal in those transition periods as they are about harvesting more value from existing assets while simultaneously stepping out into the market place that is yet not well or fully understood.

Edging strategies also contribute to financial performance. Later in *Edge Strategy: A new mindset for profitable growth*, Lewis and McKone explain: "Edge achievers have increased risk-adjusted shareholder returns by more than 15 percent versus their peers. Furthermore, these companies have outgrown their peers by 39 percent (42)".

Transforming from the edge requires retraining and/or the reallocation of resources (people, products, manufacturing capabilities, supply chain capabilities, etc.) in addition to adapting the organization to the new rules of the game. If you want to tap into the IoT opportunity and your company is an established analog player, then this strategy should be studied. It enables organizations to mix both their existing analog business and operations with the needed transformation resulting from the digital evolution of the market place. Analog specificities such as intellectual property, customer base, unique value proposition are your safe heaven guardians'. They must be leveraged to help your organization leap ahead all the newcomers that will have to bear high costs to assemble even a portion of those assets.

The Time is Now

Incumbents will need to transform themselves into digital enterprises if they want to survive. Getting digital is not all about investing in the latest technologies; more importantly, it's about setting a strategy with proper timing and dedicating the proper digital capabilities (people, business plans, operations, etc.). Not trying to understand and adapt to the new rules of the game has an impact. We have seen such impacts in market places facing digitization; companies that once were prominent in their analog market facing low margins or commoditization.

The IoT[4] strategic methodology specifically addresses the "transforming from the edge" scenario by enabling a step-by-step approach through a pragmatic methodology, helping current analog companies to avoid commoditization of their core portfolio offerings and leveraging what the IoT brings to the table, such as technologies, business models, competencies, and execution.

CHAPTER 3

DIGITIZATION STRATEGY:
THE IoT^4 METHODOLOGY

"Victorious warriors win first and then go to war, while defeated warriors go to war first and then seek to win."
Sun Tzu, The Art of War

WHY A METHODOLOGY IS NEEDED TO DEFINE IOT STRATEGIES

Today, the IoT is at the intersection of multiple trends, technologies, business models, channels, go-to-markets, and so forth.

The difficulty with the Internet of Things is that it is still under construction at the time this book is written, in 2017, not only from a standardization perspective, but also as business model and an overall competitive landscape. To prepare yourself for transferring current analog offerings into an IoT profitable and scalable offering, you need to understand how the Internet of Things will be structured and what this implies about the rules of the game and the associated threats and opportunities.

We have reviewed many studies but have never found clear answers, strong references or solid case studies on the following questions which most corporate analog leaders must consider:

- What is the IOT and how can we make my core offering more IoT-enabled?
- How can we beat the trend of commoditization that the IoT transformation will bring?
- Which marketplace can and should we play?
- What can and should we do?
- What part of our organization needs to be digitalized?
- How can we assess the level of transformation needed for our organization to leverage the IoT?

It is difficult for a company's leadership and management to be able to assess where they fit in the overall IoT competitive landscape and build a consistent plan to beat the competition and commoditization, as well as to leverage those different aspects.

THE MISSING LINK: IOT^4

To provide for the all-important answers and solutions, we have developed and defined the IoT^4 strategic methodology, which addresses all important aspects of an IoT strategy for analog companies to avoid commoditization and beat competition.

The IoT^4 methodology starts with the customers: their needs, their pain points and then clarifies different aspects of how to digitize an analog portfolio into an IoT portfolio while embracing:

- Technology: How the IoT is structuring itself from a technology perspective.
- Offering differentiation strategies: How established analog companies leverage their core offerings to avoid commoditization.
- Business models: How companies "sell" their core offerings with one-off sales or as a recurrent flow of money.
- How to transition from an analog to a digital customer experience

Each of those elements is addressed in a separate chapter of this book to give a more in-depth understanding. Merging those four concepts into a whole will give you a clear map of the strategic options and a step-by-step methodology.

IOT^4 METHODOLOGY: DEFINITION & STRUCTURE

What are we trying to solve with the IoT^4 methodology?

The objective of the methodology is to provide a series of simple and elegant steps—a reference design—for companies looking for a strategic orientation of the process. As stated before, there are the typical recurrent questions and concerns. The following is a summary:

- As we have an extended analog portfolio of products (software and hardware) and associated services, what are the elements of our core offerings and our extended portfolio which we need to adapt so to leverage what the IoT holds?
- We understand the need for open architectures and designs to leverage the IoT's ecosystems, but how does this apply to the set of products that we sell as an all-in-one system?
- There seem to be a lot of different standards; how does our core product fit into that?
- We fear commoditization due to the need to be open and compatible with numerous third parties. Which strategies can we put in place to beat commoditization and competitors?
- Should we look at new business models? If so, how does it fit with our current portfolio and go-to-market? What strategies can we put in place to leverage those new business models without putting our core business at risk?

STEP 1
Making your analog portfolio
IoT compatible

Unbundle and map your current product and software
portfolio into an IoT compatible offering using
the 6 IoT layers.

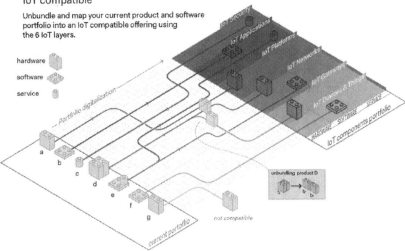

STEP 2
Defining offering differentiation strategies
in order to avoid commoditization

Strategic moves for your current portfolio that
reach beyond the technological aspects.
Integrating differentiation strategy to avoid
commoditization.

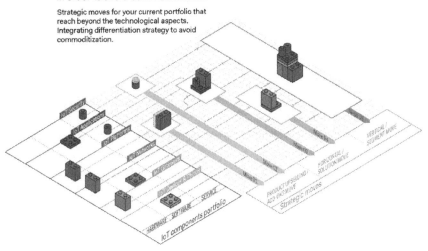

42

STEP 3

Choosing the most relevant business models

Map of where different strategic moves fit in the 5 layers of architecture and which financial model fits best.

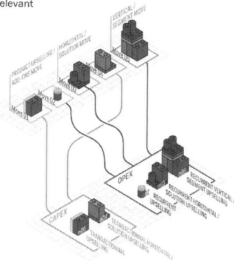

STEP 4:

From customer experience to digital savvy organizations

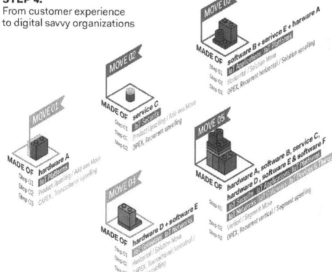

What is the IoT^4 strategic methodology?

The methodology is based on four simple steps to transition your analog portfolio to an IoT-compatible portfolio while at the same time avoiding commoditization.

The start point (Step 0) is customers. The start point is customers. The start point is not part of the four steps methodology, it is a prerequisite to the methodology. You should not start to think about a digitization strategy if you do not have a clear and defined customer centric value proposition and experience. We consider the best book is the one from Alan Smith, Alexander Osterwalder, Greg Bernarda, Gregory Bernarda, Trish Papadakos, and Yves Pigneur. Their book: Value Proposition Design: How to Create Products and Services Customers Want (44) gives a simple and pragmatic step by step methodology to express customer centric value propositions.

The next four steps are:

- First step: Making your analog portfolio IoT-compatible.
- Second step: Defining an offering differentiation strategy to avoid commoditization.
- Third step: Choosing the most relevant business models.
- Fourth step: Answering to customer needs with a unique IoT Value proposition that embraces technology, business model and avoids commoditization of your current analog portfolio. The fourth step is the summary of all previous steps. It clarifies each move which should be equal to a customer value proposition / gain. The sum of all moves should form together the targeted customer experience.

START POINT (STEP 0): CUSTOMER EXPERIENCE
Is IoT a technical subject? No, it's not.

The Internet of Things is very often understood as a way for companies to accelerate:

- their differentiation by providing unique value propositions to their customers and partners at an acceptable price.
- their financial performance.
- their employees, customers and partners' satisfaction.

All of this is true, but the final goal should be to deliver an exceptional customer experience.

It's not the technology that drives financial performance and customer satisfaction: it's the experience, the enchantment.

Guy Kawasaki, the investor, author, and former Apple "chief evangelist," in his book, Enchantment: The Art of Changing Hearts, Minds, and Actions (43); highlights that businesses must go beyond satisfying customers, they must delight them in a unique way that mixes likability, trust and products.

The starting point to the IoT^4 strategic methodology is to:

- understand your customers' pain points and benefits he expects.
- understand your current value propositions.
- identify the gaps between the current customer experience and what it should be.
- break down the gaps of your customer experience into specific "customer experience moves" that are customer centric.

FIRST STEP: MAKING YOUR ANALOG PORTFOLIO IOT-COMPATIBLE

The first IoT[4] step begins the process by addressing the IoT technology side.

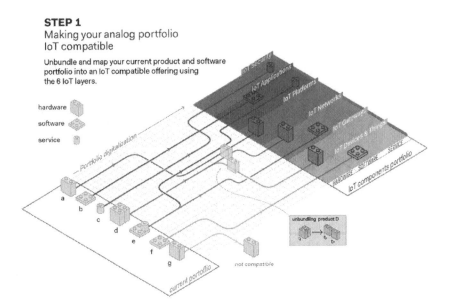

There are six different IoT layers:

- IoT Devices & Things.
- IoT Gateways.
- IoT Platforms.
- IoT users Access and Applications.
- IoT Networks (wired and wireless).
- IoT Security.

The first step relates to the technological side of the IoT and the organization in technological layers. This step is needed to assess where your core analog offerings and future IoT offerings position themselves in the technology landscape. Each level has specific requirements and constraints. As an analog company leadership team member, you need to understand which portions of your current core offerings provide the edge against your competition.

You might need to "break" or "unbundle" existing products into smaller parts to fit the IoT layers. Alternately, you can even leave some of the products of the equation if your intent is not to ever move some of your current products into the IoT, or if you wish to maintain a familiar and identifiable spot to return for loyal customers in which case you can leave out existing offers unbundled.

This step will enable you to understand the importance of each portion of your core offer, and their strengths and weaknesses when transitioning to an IoT-compatible portfolio.

SECOND STEP: DEFINING OFFERING DIFFERENTIATION STRATEGIES TO AVOID COMMODITIZATION

The second step represents all the different available options for existing analog companies to leverage their current analog core offering as well as their IoT compatible portfolio (hardware, software, and services) to avoid commoditization.

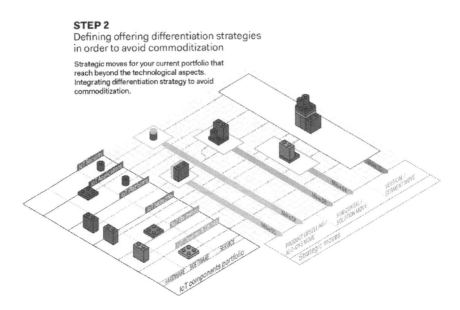

All these options are the result of adapting the "Edge Strategy™" defined by Alan Lewis and Dan McKone in their 2016 book, *Edge Strategy™: A New Mindset for Profitable Growth*, to the IoT (41):

	Edge Strategy™: beating the commoditization cycle	IoT4 strategy: Defining an offering differentiation strategy to avoid commoditization
Strategy N°1	"Edge of the product" "Edge-based customization"	Product upselling / add-ons move
Strategy N°2	"Edge-based bundling"	Horizontal / solution move
Strategy N°3	"Edge-based solutions"	Vertical / segment move

There are three strategic moves (addressed in Chapter 6) as defined below.

- Product upselling / add-ons move: Core IoT-compliant 'bricks' (with standards and non-custom-based functions) will face commoditization. These will be similar in concept to Lego bricks: standard color, standard size, standard function, and standard connectivity. This move, or option, is about how to move your core IoT component bricks into a space where customers will be willing to pay more to get a smaller extra that could fit their specific needs. These "smaller extras" can be hardware components, software add-ons, and services.
- Horizontal / solution move: This move or option is about how to bundle some of your core IoT component bricks into a space where customers are willing to pay more to find a solution across one or several layers of the IoT architecture. IoT customers will be willing to pay a higher price for simple, pre-tested integration (hardware, software, and services).
- Vertical / segment move: This move or option is about how to propose a full end-to-end unique bundle to customers ready to pay for a fully integrated system and solution.

THIRD STEP: CHOOSING THE MOST RELEVANT BUSINESS MODELS

The third step is the business model side.

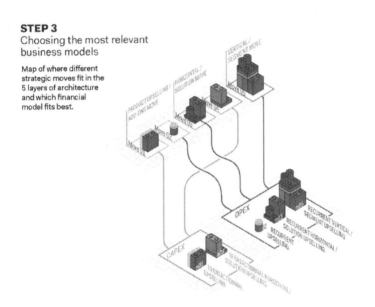

STEP 3
Choosing the most relevant business models

Map of where different strategic moves fit in the 5 layers of architecture and which financial model fits best.

As clarified in Chapter 7 there are two approaches, each with three possible moves, with the associated business models that drive differentiation:

- One-off – capex models
- Recurrent – opex models

As a result, we clearly see the emergence of six business models or moves:

Three strategic moves possible in OPEX:

- Recurrent upselling: Software add-ons – licensing, product, platforms, application sold as a service. Physical add-ons – leasing. Subscriptions – maintenance/warranty/service attached to product.
- Recurrent horizontal / solution upselling: bundling product together; system and solution as a service.
- Recurrent vertical / segment upselling: fully-integrated system and solution sold as a service. Performance, service level agreements sold as a service or as a lease.

Three strategic moves possible in CAPEX:

- Transactional upselling: software add-ons, physical add-ons
- Transactional horizontal / solution upselling: packaging systems and sold as one-off
- Transactional vertical / segment upselling: fully-integrated system and solution sold as one-off

FOURTH STEP: "CUSTOMER EXPERIENCE MOVE" AND VALUE PROPOSITION MOVES

Step 1 to 3 ensures that:

- all your current analog portfolio components are mapped in the IoT layered structure,
- you define differentiation strategies for each move,
- you have clarity on which business model apply to which move.

The fourth step is the sum of all previous steps. The fourth step gives you a map of all your individual moves. Each individual move should be equal to a customer value proposition / gain. The sum of all moves should form together the targeted customer experience.

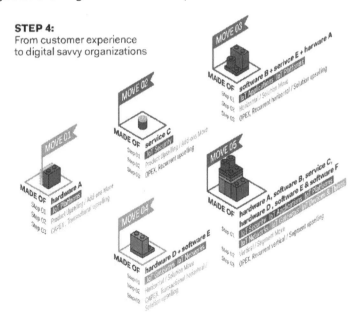

STEP 4:
From customer experience
to digital savvy organizations

In step 4 you must close the loop with the start point.

As a reminder, the starting point to the IoT^4 strategic methodology is to:

- understand your customers' pain points and benefits he expects
- understand your current value propositions
- identify the gaps between the current customer experience and what it should be
- brake down the gaps of your customer experience into specific "customer experience moves" that are customer centric

Step 4 is about looking back at your "customer experience moves" expressed in a customer centric form/value, and making sure that your IoT moves that take both technologies, business model and differentiation strategies answer your specific customer needs and pain points. This helps identifying potential gaps or incorrect placements in your portfolio as well as trigger discussions between offer managers and strategy teams to clarify the strategic intents and directions.

CHAPTER 4

IOT⁴ METHODOLOGY
STEP 0
START POINT: YOUR CUSTOMERS

"We've had three big ideas at Amazon that we've stuck with for 18 years, and they're the reason we're successful: Put the customer first. Invent. And be patient. "
Jeff Bezos

START WITH YOUR CUSTOMERS

Digitization is an enabler to better serve and bring more value to your current and future customers. If you are obsessed to solving problems for your customers, helping them in their everyday operations and being a strong contributor to their business: IoT will be an incredible opportunity for your business. Investigate what is desired and needed by your customers. Understand what the IoT is and will bring. Innovate and do not hesitate to disrupt your organization from the edge.

Showing and demonstrating a customer-centric culture and approach is the compass that guides the organization towards a successful digital transformation, leveraging both the risks and the opportunities to leapfrog the competition.

DIGITIZATION IS LIKE A CAKE

We will help you understand what the IoT may hold for you, we will explain the technologies, the business models and so forth; but you will still need to "cook" all these ingredients into your own recipe.

It is always very difficult to cook a good cake if you don't understand the possible ingredients and tools that are available to you. Understanding who are your targeted customers, what they like to eat. What they would like to eat is as important as understanding the available ingredients.

To successfully leverage the IoT, you need to start with your customers; which implies that you start with the 7 P's of the marketing mix. Interestingly those 7 P's are getting digitized as well:

- Product: digitization of portfolios with more connectivity built in
- Place: e-commerce, online ordering
- Price: online quotation
- Promotion: digital marketing through social medias, search engine optimization and so forth
- People: human interactions are getting more digitalize through video and chat features

- Processes: ordering processes are typically completely digital nowadays
- Physical Evidence: Virtual reality will become the physical evidence

Then you choose the most relevant technologies and business models to serve your targeted customers. You might also need to anticipate how this will impact your organization and processes.

IoT is a means - a tool - to bring more value to your customers. It's what you do with it that makes it valuable. Mapping your customers' journeys, problems they are trying to solve and hidden needs is your starting point to digitization; not the opposite.

"CUSTOMER EXPERIENCE MOVE" AND VALUE PROPOSITION MOVES

The objective of this book is not to repeat what other great authors have already explained: how to define customer centric value proposition and experience. We consider the best book is the one from Alan Smith, Alexander Osterwalder, Greg Bernarda, Gregory Bernarda, Trish Papadakos, and Yves Pigneur. Their book: Value Proposition Design: How to Create Products and Services Customers Want (44) gives a simple and pragmatic step by step methodology to express customer centric value propositions.

Therefore, we wanted the start point of the IoT[4] methodology to be the customer; the remaining steps are about how to translate your customer value propositions into IoT strategic moves.

We consider that the IoT is a way to serve, to enable those customer centric value propositions. Our objectives through the methodology is to explain how to digitize an existing analog portfolio to better serve your customers.

Before starting to use the IoT[4] strategic methodology, you must have done your homework and:

- understand your customers' pain points and benefits he expects.
- understand your current value propositions.
- identify the gaps between the current customer experience and what it should be.
- brake down the gaps of your customer experience into specific "customer experience moves" that are customer centric.

You should not start the first step without having a clear understanding of your "customer experience moves" expressed in a customer centric form/value. Alan Smith, Alexander Osterwalder, Greg Bernarda, Gregory

Bernarda, Trish Papadakos, and Yves Pigneur in their book Value Proposition Design: How to Create Products and Services Customers Want (44) consider that a good way to express a direction of your value proposition is to express it using this template: Our (products and services) help(s) (customer segment) who want to (jobs to be done) by (your own verb) and (your own verb). Unlike (competing value proposition).

Put your self in the shoes of your customers: this is the start point to any digital transformation. Digital transformation should not have any other purpose than to deliver unique value propositions and experience at the most efficient and maximum price that the customers will pay.

Here are some "customer experience move" simple examples:

- Our IoT enabled Home intelligent system helps house owners who want to reduce their electrical bill by reducing their electrical consumption without reducing the comfort of the house and measuring the live consumption to help the house owner to have a more diligent and proactive usage of the power. Unlike "name of a competitor" who only offers live consumption and impacts the overall comfort of the house.
- Our IoT enabled Home intelligent system helps house owners who want to have the ability to know and control what is happening by providing the ability to activate or disable what was before not feasible such as thermostats, garage door, turn off the porch light from anywhere in the world.
- Our IoT gateway and connected sensors help(s) restaurant owners who want to avoid cold food loss by ensure that the temperature of their fridge is always under a certain threshold and being informed if this happens with a fully cybersecure distant access. The restaurant owner does not want to pay for it as an investment but is ready to pay a recurrent fee for this service.

- Our IoT valves help building facility managers who want to measure and control gas and water leaks by having easy to install and fully controllable hardware by any SCADA system on the market by being fully compliant with IT and cybersecurity standards of the market.

Each individual move should be equal to a customer value proposition / gain. The sum of all moves should form together the targeted customer experience.

Once you have expressed your targeted customer experience and have clarified which possible "CUSTOMER EXPERIENCE MOVE" are needed, you can start with the step 1 of the methodology.

CHAPTER 5

IOT⁴ METHODOLOGY
STEP 1:
MAKING YOUR ANALOG PORTFOLIO IOT-COMPATIBLE

"Once a new technology rolls over you, if you're not part of the steamroller, you're part of the road."
Stewart Brand

Note for readers: For some of you this chapter is going to be a challenge, but it is a necessary pain to understand the underlying technologies to understand and master the IoT. IoT relies on technologies. If you want to understand the IoT, you must understand what hides behind the IoT acronyms such as CoAP, AEP, Thread and so forth.

I recommend that as a minimum you check the titles of each section and if you don't recognize the terminology, I suggest you read it.

I will add another note for you where the technical content begins so that you can skip the paragraphs that go into more details.

The Internet of Things is changing the rules of the game, mainly due to the impact it has on unleashing data and accelerating the speed of advancement in products, business models, time to market, and other factors.

As the IoT becomes a ubiquitous phenomenon all over the globe, these transitions may occur in a matter of weeks, days, or even hours. In fact, as this book was first being written, "Pokémon GO" was being launched. And even though this does not entail the release of an IoT product, it is an example of an application spreading like wildfire with tens of millions of installations over a matter of days. The impact on the Nintendo financials was impressive: Pokémon GO's release has almost doubled Nintendo's stock in a couple of days, adding $17.6 billion in market capitalization.

In the near future, those businesses that are willing to confront the new digital world and adapt promptly have good chances to survive and prosper. Those which do not pivot fast enough will wither and possibly disappear.

- **Hardware companies** that have been developing and manufacturing analog products and/or legacy systems will face challenges in making those portfolios IoT-compatible. IoT will bring the commoditization of portions of existing profitable portfolios and the cannibalization of channels. It is vital for CTOs and associate leaders to understand what IoT means in terms of impact, not only from a pure technological side, but also from an ecosystem, go-to-market, and business model view. If those companies seek to produce complete solutions for their customers, create technology which gives distinct advantages to make their product lines more attractive, and work to keep costs down and remain competitive while still making a profit and understanding and influencing the way IoT standards are being defined, their future success is almost guaranteed.
- **Software companies** can take advantage of the many opportunities in IoT for application development. The IoT brings

great opportunities in the fields of IoT platforms, vertical applications, analytics, and security. The immense quantity of data creates huge requirements for management of information, storage, and analysis through advanced analytics and artificial intelligence. Additionally, software will be needed to connect as a meeting point (IoT platforms) but also to control, monitor, and react to the IoT stream of information shared by "smart things."

What is the current landscape of IoT technologies? To make it simple: it is still the Wild, Wild West. There are no standards, no global IoT interoperability certifications, and no leader on IoT platforms. All of this is still to come. There remain many challenges that need to be to overcome in the coming years inside and outside of the IoT. This includes products and software, such as how to deal with scalability, how to secure transactions when handling so many things and people wanting to interact with many things and people, and how to monetize and efficiently deal with service management on such a scale. Therefore understanding what IoT is today is so critical for software and hardware vendors.

IoT's main contribution is the unleashing all available data in order to leverage it. But IoT is a technical subject relying heavily on standards, protocols, and architectures. We will address all those aspects of the IoT, including technologies, standards, and protocols, as well as existing solutions to deal with speed and innovation.

IOT BASICS
Because there are currently no defined, deployed, and global standards, we felt it was important to go back to the three laws that you can refer to when wondering where the trends are heading. The difficulty with this enormous uptake in digitally connected objects and people is to gain clarity on the identified rules that govern those trends. These three laws provide a good understanding of what is in store for the future:

Kurzweil's Law

The speed of change as well as processing speed is accelerating.

According to Kurzweil's Law of Accelerating Returns (45), change in evolutionary systems tends to increase exponentially.

In *'The Age of Spiritual Machines'*, Kurzweil also adds that: "An analysis of the history of technology shows that technological change is exponential, contrary to the common-sense 'intuitive linear' view. So we won't experience just the actual 100 years of progress in the 21st century—it will be more like 20,000 years of progress (at today's rate). The 'returns,' such as chip speed and cost-effectiveness, also increase exponentially. Within a few decades, machine intelligence will surpass human intelligence (45)".

If you look at the speed of adoption, to get an 80 percent ownership and overall technology adaption, it took the following number of years for each of those technologies:

- Car: 110 years
- Telephone and airplane: 75 years
- Electricity: 70 years
- Radio, VCR: 40 years
- TV: 30 years

Essentially, Kurzweil's Law, when applied to the IoT, indicates that current analog companies that have very often settled and built their offer portfolio and associated market shares gradually over numerous years will be dealing with an acceleration of momentum. Due to technology evolutions, new companies are hunting their customers with disruptive product and business models, and the impact of this is very often underestimated. The speed at which manufacturers, software editors, channels, and end users are trying to surf the IoT wave is impressive.

Metcalfe's Law

Connecting "things" into a network brings more value than those individual things do when taken separately.

Metcalfe's Law indicates that in a communication network of n members, you will end up with potentially $n(n-1)/2$ connections between each of those participants. If you consider that each connection between those members is of an equal value, you end up with a total value of the telecommunications network to the square of the number of connected users of the system ($n2$). This means that the bigger your network, the value of being connected to it grows exponentially while the cost per user remains the same or even reduces. The limit of this law is that it considers, as a hypothesis, that each connection is at the same value and that connectivity and interoperability are seamless (46).

Essentially, Metcalfe's Law, when applied to the IoT, indicates that if you connect two smart things or people, then they will be able to communicate with each other, creating increased value. If you, in the same way, begin to connect billions of devices, people, and associated applications, then the overall value created rises exponentially and dramatically.

Gilder's Law

There will be more communication bandwidth available.

According to George Gilder, from his book 'Telecosm: How Infinite Bandwidth Will Revolutionize Our World' (47), an American investor, writer, economist and techno-utopian advocate, the total bandwidth of communication systems triples every nine to twelve months.

Essentially, Gilder's Law, when applied to the IoT, indicates that it is realistic to think that the available bandwidth resource will be abundant. Certainly, the IoT does require bandwidth but, more importantly, it depends on global availability of bandwidth more than the absolute value of bandwidth (small objects may be connected in areas where there was previously very scarce access).

In summary, there are plenty of laws out there but those three laws, when applied to the IoT context, enable you to understand in an easy way where the IoT comes from in a technological sense, and where it is heading. They imply that the IoT is a natural progression of the M2M evolution that started in the early 2000s, and that it will benefit from:

- More bandwidth available.
- More value brought by more connected objects, people, etc.
- More speed in the technology's definition, implementation, and usage.

COST OF GOODS

The IT market has been experiencing a drop in the cost of goods for many years. This is a global trend that will also apply to the IoT. The performance of available computing resources such as memory, CPUs, and disk drives has increased dramatically while the size and price has dropped at the same time. This is illustrated by the growth of the personal computer. When they first came out in the 1980s, personal computers were slow, had tiny amounts of memory and disk space, and were very large and bulky. The first cellular phones had the same characteristics: very small screens, very low memory, and few functions. Compare this with the computer that most people now carry in their pocket--their smartphone--which is not only blindingly fast, has a large amount of memory, proportionately costs very little, and is small enough to fit into a pocket or even on a wristwatch.

Today, in the age of mobility, virtually everyone owns more than one computer. Most people have a smart phone—which is a computer—and perhaps a small laptop or tablet, as well as others scattered all over their office or home in the form of smart devices. Additionally, people can control all their computing resources from one system, performing complex tasks with a few keystrokes and simple commands. For example,

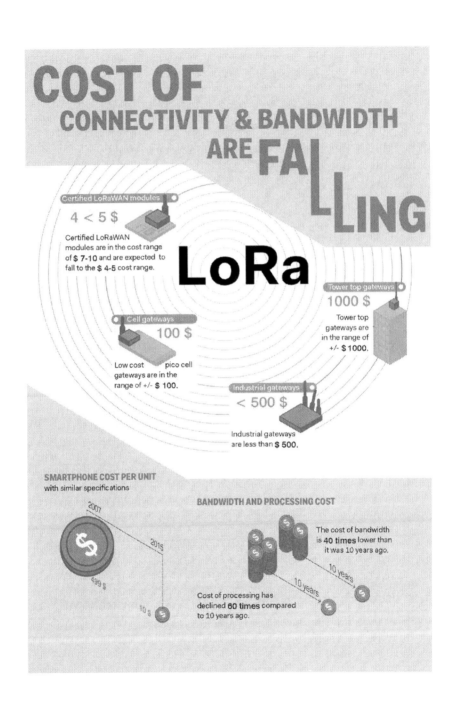

COST OF
CONNECTIVITY & BANDWIDTH
ARE FALLING

Certified LoRaWAN modules

4 < 5 $

Certified LoRaWAN modules are in the cost range of $ 7-10 and are expected to fall to the $ 4-5 cost range.

LoRa

Tower top gateways

1000 $

Tower top gateways are in the range of +/- $ 1000.

Cell gateways

100 $

Low cost pico cell gateways are in the range of +/- $ 100.

Industrial gateways

< 500 $

Industrial gateways are less than $ 500.

SMARTPHONE COST PER UNIT
with similar specifications

2007

2015

499 $

10 $

BANDWIDTH AND PROCESSING COST

The cost of bandwidth is **40 times** lower than it was 10 years ago.

10 years

10 years

Cost of processing has declined **60 times** compared to 10 years ago.

72

COST OF TECHNOLOGY IS FALLING

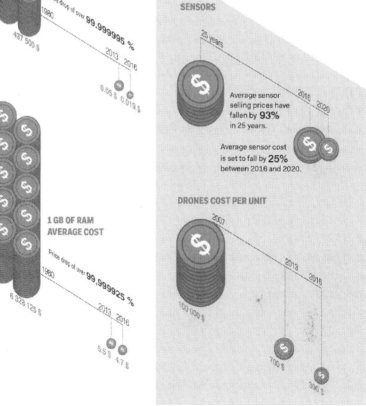

1GB OF HARD DISK MEMORY COST

Price drop of over **99.999995 %**

1980

437 500 $

2013 2016

0.05 $ 0.019 $

1 GB OF RAM AVERAGE COST

Price drop of over **99.999925 %**

1980

6 328 125 $

2013 2016

5.5 $ 4.7 $

SENSORS

25 years

Average sensor selling prices have fallen by **93%** in 25 years.

Average sensor cost is set to fall by **25%** between 2016 and 2020.

2016 2020

DRONES COST PER UNIT

2007

100 000 $

2013 2016

700 $ 300 $

a robot vacuum cleaner, robot mop, and smart light bulbs can all be programmed and maintained from a simple tablet device.

As you can see, the pace of change for computing resources is moving forward at a dramatic rate. The implications of these changes as we consider the future are astounding. Smart devices connected to the Internet of Things are appearing everywhere, from homes to businesses to factories and beyond. More and more businesses will be affected by these changes in technology as the price of computing resources continues to drop, the computing power continues to increase, and the energy requirements shrink.

IoT will benefit from this and it will, in fact, be a core success and acceleration factor. IoT's speed of integration by manufacturers and software editors is being driven amazingly fast by low prices combined with high performances.

If you add the smaller power requirements and associated technologies which harvest the environment's available power to the increase in capabilities and the associated reduced cost of the components of today's and tomorrow's IoT, then you have all the necessary prerequisites for a major transformation.

Power consumption is predicted to decrease dramatically. An analysis of the change in energy usage over the last fifty years shows that the electrical efficiency of computers has doubled approximately every one and a half years (48). Assuming the trend continues, power consumption, even with a tenfold increase in the number of devices, would be reduced by a factor of ten.

Therefore, we expect that the implementation of the Internet of Things as a connected global network of devices and people to accelerate in the coming decade. IoT network expansion is happening now and is inevitable. Standards do and will play an important role in the speed at which the IoT technologies are being spread amongst the industries and associated ecosystems, as well as how interoperability will bring the end user added value.

IOT STANDARDS

Standardization is one of the most critical hurdles of the IoT evolution. Without global standards, the complexity of devices that need to connect and communicate with each other (with all the associated addressing, automation, quality of service, interfaces, data repository and associated directory services, etc.) will grow exponentially. The IoT promises billions of connected things which in turn require common standards in order to operate with an acceptable, manageable and scalable level of complexity.

Why is IoT standardization important?

Let's take a simple transaction: data is typically collected by sensors within IoT devices, transmitted via wireless and wired networks to data and application warehouses virtualized in the cloud, and aggregated for analysis to determine information such as usage patterns through analytics and business intelligence applications. Standardizing is not particularly important to solve interoperability, as this can always be achieved through multiprotocol gateways. Standardization across the IoT landscape is important because this reduces the gaps between protocols (and associated security holes and issues). It also reduces the overall cost of data, associated transport costs and the cost of manufacturing of individual components. This is because fewer standards enable more compatible components, which all leads to reduced cost of design, manufacturing and a reduced time to market. Standardization also streamlines the overall integration at an application level (aggregation of data, interoperability of data, reports and business processes) without being concerned with individual IT devices, unique protocols and non-standard data formats.

Why are IoT regulations important?

Regulations and voluntary compliance is required to clarify the ownership of data, how and under what conditions it may be sold or shared, how it is collected, requirements for privacy, and how the information is manipulated. The amount of data created by devices and people in the coming years will be so important that it will reveal that data has no legal boundaries. For example, data can be generated in Spain, stored in

Thailand, backed up in Australia and used by analytics running on a virtualized server in the USA.

In another example, handling medical data in the United States requires strict compliance to the HIPPA laws which state that medical data may not be shared without the permission of the patient. This introduces legal issues when the location of many of the components' storing, analyzing and transmitting data is not known.

Let's consider smart and connected cars, and some of the questions in that area that need to be addressed:

- Will the police have access to the data repository within a smart car – which maintains a GPS record of everywhere it's been, what speeds it's traveled, and the driver's habits? This becomes even more interesting when you consider that some cars have dash, rear and even internal cameras recording the passenger and driver conversations and actions.
- Will a search warrant be required to obtain this information, even if it has been transmitted into the cloud and no longer exists on the car itself?
- How must the data be secured?
- Do the owners of smart cars have any rights over the usage of the data originating from their car?

This becomes complicated when multiple devices communicate with each other, with various data aggregators, and with multiple command and control stations across different countries and associated jurisdictions and laws. In the world of telemedicine, which heavily depends upon connectivity, medical devices could be operated from within the patient's room as well as from a central location in the hospital, and possibly even from a remote location on the other side of the planet. Standards are vital to allow these devices to operate with each other, with a physician's tablet in another country, and within the hospital control system. Additionally, since the information is privileged and private, regulatory standards are required to ensure the data remains secure, and to specify the ownership and under what conditions that it can be released to others.

The Importance of Influencing Standardization Organizations and Alliances

Until now, a few large organizations have been responsible for the definition of the M2M protocols or have performed the needed research and development, and the market presence to enforce those standards. This has created a multiplicity of M2M stacks and ecosystems with very limited interoperability. The current M2M related standards landscape is a result of that: it is highly fragmented. This can be seen across domains where only basic communication and networking standards are being used. There is a trend to increase coordination work done to define a common IoT stack by the different international standard organizations such as ETSI, IEEE, IETF, CEN/ISO, CENELEC/IEC, ITU-T, OASIS, OGC and onem2m. But there is still a long road ahead of us. The beauty of what IoT promises is a seamless interoperability between things, gateways, applications and users that will enable scalability, cross things added value applications, services and cost optimization (49).

You could represent the M2M market as closed standards landscape with very few interoperability capabilities.

In an IoT landscape you enable all those closed systems to interconnect with one another.

It is vital to understand the importance of standards and the protocols that your current products will need to comply with.

The capacity for analog companies to influence standards to their own benefit is an important aspect when dealing with commoditization. Lines of Businesses in Analog companies that have not been used to influence Standardization organizations should, once they have clarified their strategy in dealing with IoT and their core offer, make sure they proactively drive the standards to their benefit. In the IT world, influencing standards has been a well-known game for decades. Unfortunately, companies that have been working in vertical segments or with legacy protocols will be facing a painful learning curve and they might miss some important steps when protecting their investments in R&D.

Note for readers: The following paragraphs will be highly technical. If you don't want to go into this level of details I suggest you go to the summary of this chapter.

IOT STANDARDIZATION: CURRENT STATE

Many of the modern standards for the Internet do not suffice for supporting IoT efficiently and economically, since IoT didn't exist, even as a concept, when those protocols were designed and implemented. Additionally, since the infrastructure for IoT throughout the world has not been fully developed, many IoT devices have been implemented with proprietary protocols, making it difficult for them to communicate with one another. However, as more companies enter the world of the digital revolution, they will push hard for standardization so they can focus on providing services rather than developing proprietary hardware and software.

Currently, many connected devices do not work well together because they have not been designed by the Research and Development teams with a cross protocol interoperability mindset. For example, medical IOT devices should ideally work with one another for the patients benefit. Thus, the heart monitor would be aware of the breathing monitor which in turn, would be aware of the Smart IV so that adjustments could be made automatically to a patient's intravenous drug regimen as needed. In the current world, these devices operate independently, but as standards are developed, they could communicate with each other to create an environment where patient care is more optimal.

There are hundreds, if not thousands, of different technologies currently in existence, and these use a wide variety of different protocols, networking technologies, and buses. Even if more and more devices tend to communicate via IP and very often leverage, on top of it, legacy or proprietary protocols, it is vital that these standards be globally accepted, since IoT devices will be installed all over the planet. Unfortunately, the current state is not creating enough of a need for the development of protocol bridges and gateways so that they can integrate and operate together.

The standardization of the IoT can be characterized more by an evolution from existing standards into an orchestrated methodology. This, in turn, will create the conditions for more interoperability, connectivity, "digital trust" with blockchain technologies and artificial intelligence distribution between heterogeneous components and systems.

In summary, IoT standards are still wide open and 'wild west', as there are no global validated standardization frameworks at the IoT stack level. There will be an exponential increase in the number and types of smart devices over the next decade. One of the biggest challenges, upon which the eventual success of IoT is dependent, is the development of interoperable global standards. Without enforcement of standards, the value and commercial viability of IoT will not reach its full potential.

Interestingly, the current gap and associated need to find a solution in interoperability has opened huge opportunities for software bridging those gaps: IoT platforms. We see more and more IoT platforms making the promise of interoperability into a scalable and sustainable matter; at the same time, this opens interoperability questions between those platforms. This will be addressed later in this document.

OneM2M

OneM2M is a global standards initiative formed in 2012. The architecture it defines is a simple, 3 layers, architecture (network, service and application).

OneM2M seems is well on track to become the actual network intermediation framework standard. An assessment of the current available whitepapers and specifications while I write this book will already be outdated when this book will be published. I therefore highly recommend you regularly get updates from their website: http://www.onem2m.org

OSI model

To leverage the IoT, one must understand the foundations it uses to solve the interoperability challenge. Unfortunately for readers with little technical background, it is necessary to go through the learning curve to understand how to leverage it. We will not be going into details regarding this topic, as there is plenty of literature available if you want more information.

Communication systems have solved this hurdle by using a set of rules and standards to format data and control data exchange. The most common methodology used in the telecom industry is the Open Systems Interconnection (OSI) model designed in the 1970's (people sometimes don't know about or remember the standardization war that happened between CII-Honeywell-Bull, DEC and IBM.) The OSI network model separates a communication into layers which allows easier implementation.

The purpose of the Open Systems Interconnection reference model is to provide a common basis for the coordination of standards development for system interconnection. The basic structuring technique in the Reference Model of Open Systems Interconnection is layering. According to this technique, each open system is viewed as logically composed of an ordered set of (N)-subsystems (50).

The OSI network model has 7 layers:

- Layer 7: The application layer.
- Layer 6: The presentation layer.
- Layer 5: The session layer.
- Layer 4: The transport layer.
- Layer 3: The network layer.
- Layer 2: The data-link layer.
- Layer 1: The physical layer.

TCP/IP model

TCP/IP means Transmission Control Protocol and Internet Protocol. It is the model currently used as the basic communication language of the Internet and similar IT networks. Technical standards are maintained by the Internet Engineering Task Force (IETF) (51) (52).

The TCP/IP model which has 4 layers, based the OSI model, is used for data communication on the internet. Each layer in the model corresponds to one or more layers of the seven-layer Open Systems Interconnection (OSI) model:

OSI MODEL	TCP/IP MODEL
Application Layer	Application Layer
Presentation Layer	
Session Layer	
Transport Layer	Transport Layer
Network Layer	Internet Layer
Data Link Layer	Network Access Layer
Physical Layer	

When zooming into the TCP/IP model, you can find well known protocols:

WEB STACK

TCP/IP	Web applications
Data Format	HTML, XML, JSON
Application Layer	HTTP, DHCP, DNS, TLS/SSL
Transport Layer	TCP, UDP
Internet Layer	IPv6, IPv4, IPSec
Network/Link Layer	Ethernet (IEEE 802.3), DSL, ISDN, WIreless LAN (IEEE 802.11), Wi-Fi

The protocol that ties everything together is the ubiquitous IP, and there are two versions:

- IPv4 - the earlier form of the protocol (first described in 1980) can address about 234 addresses, and most of those already been used. As H Chaouchi states in his book "IPV4 was not designed for the Internet of Things (53)".
- IPv6 – is the most recent version (first description in 1998). IPv4, has made the transition to IPv6 unavoidable. The Google's figures are revealing an IPv6 adoption rate following an exponential curve, doubling every 9 months (54). IPv6 is being adopted by numerous Internet providers and hardware manufacturers (55). IPv6 enables a wide adoption and use of IP addresses needed by the IoT. It can provide up to 2128 unique addresses, which represents 3.4 × 1038 addresses. In other words, more than 2 billion of billions addresses per square millimeter of the Earth surface. It is quite sufficient to address the needs of any present and future communicating device (54).

IPv6 is replacing the older IPv4 protocol. For the foreseeable future, both IPv4 and IPv6 will remain in use throughout the internet. You can find the latest IPV6 adoption on http://6lab.cisco.com/stats/

IPv6 and IoT

The main challenge with the TCP/IP stack, since it was designed for the internet, is that it does not handle the constraints brought on by the Internet of Things in the most efficient manner. These constraints include small objects with low available power and low power consumption, needing to connect with low available bandwidth, and delivering low data connection on a scarce wireless network.

The European IoT6 research project is a 3 years FP7 European research project on the Internet of Things. It aims at exploring the potential of IPv6 and related standards (6LoWPAN, CORE, COAP, etc.) to overcome the current shortcomings and fragmentation of the Internet of Things (56).

They have designed and tested a protocol suite enabling the integration of multiple communication protocols into an architecture.

The research project has collaborated with several international standardizations bodies such as:

- The Institute of Electrical and Electronics Engineers (IEEE) is a non-profit organization formed in 1963. The IEEE Standards Association has a portfolio of over 1,100 active standards and more than 500 standards under development including the prominent IEEE 802® standards for local, metropolitan, and other area networks, including Ethernet and Wireless LAN (commonly referred to as Wi-Fi®). There are more than 421,000 members in more than 160 countries (57).
- The Internet Engineering Task Force (IETF) is an open standard organization formed in 1986. IETF is an organized activity of the Internet Society which is a non-profit organization founded in 1992 to provide leadership in Internet-related standards, education, and policy (58). IETF is particularly responsible for the TCP/IP suite. IETF specifications (drafts and final versions) are published as "request for comments" (RFCs).
- The ITU Telecommunication Standardization Sector (ITU-T) was formed in 1865 as a body standardizing international telegraph exchange. The ITU-T is one of the three sectors of the International Telecommunication Union (ITU) which is the United Nations specialized agency for information and communication technologies. ITU-T coordinates standards for telecommunications through study groups which develop and release standards recommendations.
- OASIS (Advancing open standards for the information society) is a non-profit consortium founded in 1993 by vendors and users wanting to have guidelines among products that supported the Standard Generalized Markup Language. It now has more than 5000 participants in more than 65

countries. OASIS releases standards for multiple usages such as Smart Grid, IoT/M2M, Big Data and so forth (59).

The European IoT6 research project has gathered some key recommendations on how to exploit IPv6 features for the IoT in their "Integration handbook for SMEs" available on their website: www IoT6.eu.

They consider that the main benefits of IPv6 for the IoT are the following: (60)

- Scalability
- Enabling the extension of the Internet and the web of things
- Solving the NAT barrier
- Improving Routing
- StateLess Address AutoConfiguration
- Multicast and anycast
- Quality of Service
- Mobility
- Security
- IPv6 version available for low-power devices
- Fully Internet compliant

Taking into consideration the fact that IoT objects need very low power consumptions and optimized transmission of "unneeded data, protocol overhead, and non-optimized communication patterns", they have proposed and clarified an IoT architecture and the following level (61):

- Device Level: devices leveraging IPv6 and legacy devices leveraging specific protocols, such as KNX, ZigBee, or Bluetooth, as well as IPv4.
- Communication Level: Devices are connected either via the so-called half gateways (that convert legacy protocols to IPv6) or directly, when they are IPv6-enabled.

- Service Level: the IoT6 architecture support several solutions for service registration and discovery.

Other standardization groups are also contributing to the standards of the IoT such as:

- International Organization for Standardization (ISO) is an independent non-governmental organization of national standards bodies (individuals or companies cannot become members).

In conclusion of this paragraph and to summarize:

- IPV6 is a reliable solution to address the specific requirements (scalability, interoperability, multicast and anycast, etc.) of the IoT
- IoT is likely to keep a certain level of heterogeneity including several communication protocols.
- IoT is likely to integrate all this heterogeneous landscape into IPv6
- IPv6 is part of a wider IoT architecture including complementary standards

IoT acronyms

Here are some clarifications of important acronyms to know when speaking about the technical side of the IoT:

Interoperability and communication protocols:
- IEEE 802.15.4: Low Rate WPAN. These Wireless Personal Area Networks enable interoperability and communication between portable and mobile computing devices such as PCs, Smartphones, electronic tablets, peripherals, cell phones and consumer electronics (62). One of the objectives of the Low Rate WPAN is to enable low data rate solution between those

devices with multi-month to multi-year battery life as well as keeping the complexity at a low level. IEEE 802.15.4 operates in unlicensed international frequency bands for IoT devices such as sensors, smart badges, actuators, controls and home automation (63). The IEEE 802.15.4 has undergone multiple releases and variants to adapt to different forms of physical layers and applications. It is the standard used by other specifications such as ZigBee, 6lowPAN, ISA100.11a and Thread. Those specifications extend the current standard by specifying some upper layers.

- IETF 6loWPAN: an acronym for IPv6 over Low Power Wireless Personal Area Networks, enhances IPv6 to support the communication requirements of low-power devices and IEEE 802.15.4 networks and is a compressed version of IPv6 (64). 6loWPAN is how you do IPV6 over low-power networks which is typically one of the constraints that IoT devices have (65).

Routing protocols:
- IETF RPL: IPv6 Routing Protocol for Lowpower and Lossy Networks (LLNs). LLNs are networks in which routers are constraints due to processing power, memory, and energy (battery power); as well as their interconnects that are characterized by high loss rates, low data rates, and instability. These networks can range from small numbers of routers (in the range of 10) to large network made of thousands of routers. These networks can be point to point type of connection to full meshed multipoint architectures (66).

Messaging protocols:
- IETF CoAP: Constrained Application Protocol. It's a web transfer protocol meeting (like HTTP, which is not the most adapted to the IoT constraints) adapted to very low overhead, and simplicity for constrained environments (67).

- ISO MQTT: Message Queuing Telemetry Transport. MQTT is a Client Server publish/subscribe messaging transport protocol. It is light weight, open, simple, and designed to be easy to implement and used in constrained environments that require small code footprint or limited bandwidth (68).
- IETF XMPP: Extensible Messaging and Presence Protocol enables streaming of Extensible Markup Language (XML) elements in close to real time between any two network endpoints and is used mainly for the purpose of building instant messaging and presence applications that meet the requirements of RFC 2779 (69).
- ISO AMQP: Advanced Message Queuing Protocol defines a binary wire-level protocol, meaning that the data is sent as a stream of bytes and therefore can be created or read by any tool that comply with this format. Unlike HTTP and XMPP, AMQP does not have a standard API (70).

IoT stack

The diagram below shows a simple IoT stack leveraging the TCP/IP model and how the IoT stack seems to be structuring itself. There is still a lot of discussions among numerous standardization organizations to get the most adapted IoT stack to the use that markets will make from it. We might be ending up with different stacks depending on the nature of the usage it answers. This gives you a good representation of how the IoT is structuring itself:

	IOT STACK		WEB STACK
TCP/IP	IOT applications	Device Management	Web applications
Data Format	Binary, JSON, CBOR		HTML, XML, JSON
Application Layer	CoAP, MQTT, XMPP, AMPQP		HTTP, DHCP, DNS, TLS/SSL
Transport Layer	UDP, DTLS		TCP, UDP
Internet Layer	IPv6/IP Routing		IPv6, IPv4, IPSec
	6LOWPAN		
Network/Link Layer	IEEE 802.15.4 MAC		Ethernet (IEEE 802.3), DSL, ISDN, WIreless LAN (IEEE 802.11), Wi-Fi
	IEEE 802.15.4 PHY / Physical Radio		

At the time this book was written, the current landscape of standardization groups, associations, and organizations is still being influenced by the different stakeholders. Standards are a core component of not only the success of the IoT as a trend, but more importantly as a weapon for companies to win the speed war of time to market.

IoT stack compliance

An important aspect of standardization when focusing on analog companies wanting to move their current product portfolio to the IoT space is to understand that neither the IETF, nor the IEEE, run certification programs. This very often causes challenges for vendors and manufacturers who want to get official recognition that their products comply with any of the standards released by both organizations.

Other organizations leverage the defined standards from IEEE and IETF to create certification programs. IEEE Conformity Assessment Program (ICAP) falls into this category. ICAP is not a Test Laboratory but will partner with industry leading test laboratories to deliver robust conformity assessment programs (71). Another example is the Wi-Fi Alliance that was formed in 1999 to certify Wi-Fi products indicating that they have met industry-agreed standards for interoperability, security, and a range of application specific protocols (72). Very often application, network range, network topology, power source and throughout drive those other organizations to publish their own IoT "implementation" of those standards.

IOT STACK: FUTURE STATE AND ASSOCIATE LAYERED ARCHITECTURE

The internet of things will change the rules of the game and will change the basis of competition in the manufacturing space.

Today's manufacturers that want to strategize their IoT approach will need to choose where they will want to play and compete. Moving an existing analog portfolio into an IoT compatible offer by leveraging the IT layered architecture framework is an important step into digitization.

Current analog manufacturers are becoming aware of the fact that they need to make their current portfolio more IoT compatible and this will push them to choose their battles knowing which rules apply for which layer (hardware, software, and services). Some players will want to play only in one layer (sensors providers, gateways manufacturers, and platform providers) while others might choose to provide end-to-end solutions.

Some IoT suppliers will choose to play on a single layer and therefore go for the high-volume, low-cost approach. Others will choose to implement specific added value functions or services enabling them to go for lower volume with higher customization and therefore avoiding the communization war.

In this chapter, we are proposing a simple way to understand the future state of the IoT and how it will structure itself to move an existing analog portfolio into an IoT compatible offer. One critical challenge, for the analog manufacturers, once they understand where they fit in the overall IoT architecture, will be to find ways to create and capture value. The value will shift from Products to systems, from Systems to Data, from Data to Knowledge, From Knowledge to Services. Therefore, one who wants to leverage the IoT to transform its core analog offering needs to understand the 5-layers architecture.

IoT: The 6 Layers Architecture

Due to the complexity of the IoT environment, which is worldwide, it's necessary to look at it from a high level and understand the various layers of which it is comprised. There might be one "standard IoT" stack; there might be several co-existing (as described above); nevertheless, IoT will structure itself into layers very like the OSI model and with adaptation needed to cope with IoT needs, constraints and usages. The need for interoperability will see an increasing market evolve around IoT Labs, facilities or IoT testbeds.

We consider that there will be mainly 6 layers; each of these layers contains distinct technology, software and devices which is a mix of legacy and more advanced hardware and software. Layering the IoT enables people to easily understand where a technology or a product sits.

What guides our thoughts are the same principals used to determine the seven layers in the OSI Reference Model.

The following principles have been used to determine the seven layers in the Reference Model and are felt to be useful for guiding further decisions in the development of OSI standards (50):

a) Keep the engineering simple by limiting the number of layers.
b) Minimize the interactions between layers.
c) Ensure each layer addresses different functions.
d) Group functions that perform similar tasks into the same layer.
e) Design functions in each layer to be able to redesign them without impacting other layers.
f) Standardize interfaces.

Consequently, we consider that the IoT will be defined through 6 layers: four vertical and two transversals:

Vertical:
1. IoT Devices & Things.
2. IoT Gateways.
3. IoT Platforms.
4. IoT users Access and Applications.

Transversals:
5. IoT Networks (wired and wireless).
6. IoT Security.

We go into details in each of those layers in the following paragraphs

Layer 1 - IoT Devices & Things

The most obvious layer is the physical thing or device (Objects, Sensors, actuators, displays, meters and so forth), which is commonly what the consumer purchases from their local electronics store or online. An example might be in the consumer world a smart refrigerator, a smart lightbulb, or smart house alarm system. It would also be, as a further example, in the enterprise world a HVAC (Heating, Ventilation and Air-Conditioning) system, the valves, actuators and sensors.

When designing an IoT device or making your core analog offering evolve into the IoT space, it is important to consider that the IoT device might work as standalone thing or as an individual contributor of a larger network. There are different ways a thing could be connected into the rest of the IOT infrastructure and objects:

- Direct connectivity between the thing and the IoT platform
- Connected thru a mesh of other IoT things (that could afterwards leverage an IoT gateway if needed)
- Connected to an IOT gateway
- No connectivity

One of the most exciting developments in the world of IoT is that the cost of components is and will continue coming down dramatically in the coming years. The cost of connectivity and the cost of security will also be going down. The fact that all of those "IoT Things" will unleash a huge quantity of data/information will enable businesses to use real-time data as it is captured by thousands, millions and even billions of devices. This is for us the real true impact of IoT that enables new business models, new markets, and so forth.

On the other side, manufacturers wanting to play in this portion of the IoT will face commoditization. IOT suppliers that seek to position themselves on this layer will need to provide one of the following:

- Basic IoT blocks: specialize in very basic technology and providing standardized basic IoT things at a very reasonable price. The maxim of small pieces, loosely joined, should be followed when designing infrastructure, devices and applications. This will allow more generalized IoT components to be used in a greater variety of ways than was originally designed. An important aspect of those standardized IoT Things will be their openness towards developers to localize or customize those standardized IoT components. This allows applications to be created using prebuilt and predesigned modules and libraries which can be obtained at little to no cost.
- Customized or special-purpose IoT blocks: develop industry-vertical specific IoT Things addressing specific needs, functions, environment conditions, etc. For example, specific temperature sensors for harsh environments such as oil platforms. Customers would be willing to pay more for those specific, customized IoT things.

Is there a way to answer, elegantly, all those constraints? Where is the IoT thing layer heading?

LittleBits Electronics is a startup, designing small circuit boards with each delivering simple functions. Their official definition is that "LittleBits™ is a platform of easy-to-use electronic building blocks that empower you to invent anything, from your own remote-controlled car to a smart home device. The Bits snap together with magnets, no soldering, no wiring, no programming needed (73)". The interesting part of what they are trying to achieve is to build a whole library of simple, basic blocks. If you extend it to the world of IoT and IoT things, we think that this is where the overall industry will be going because it answers the multiple constraints in a simple way:

Basic IoT blocks:
- simple individual blocks enabling answers one or multiple IoT things characteristics.
- reduce cost because there are very basic function blocks that can be used in multiple applications enabling manufacturers to have volume with limited SKUs (Stock Keeping Unit).
- open source and openness enabling ecosystems of developers and third-party manufacturers.
- infinite combinations answering the complexity of customization and localization

Customized or special-purpose IoT blocks:
- could be the sum of some of those basic blocks.
- could have specific manufacturers not willing to go for the basic block commoditization market but ready to invest in specific IoT blocks that would answer the return on investment of such blocks.

If the IoT goes down that path of unitary "Blocks", this will lead to the logical next steps which would be IoT devices / unitary "blocks" requirements. To give a bit of clarity on what would typically be IoT devices requirements, the list below what we consider the most important and relevant (20):
- Reliable: It is vital that IoT devices are designed and manufactured to be reliable and robust due to the need for longevity and performance.
- Reasonable to Low cost: It is essential that cost be kept at a reasonable level for IoT devices and that the balance between cost and benefit be well adapted for each usage and market. As detailed in the beginning of this chapter, things (if not designed specifically for dedicated vertical markets) will be costing less and less at an equivalent set of functionalities.
- Low power consumption & energy harvesting (when applicable): we will be seeing more and more standalone devices harvest their power source from their Environment

(light, temperature, vibrations, etc.). The value to end users on a reduced total cost of ownership for that equipment will be so important that environmental energy harvesting might become a de facto standard in the area of IoT devices (at least on those delivering low level of functions such as temperature sensors).

- Optimal and adaptive set of features: even though it makes sense that the IoT structures itself in unitary "blocks", the consumers and businesses will not tolerate, and cannot afford, to deal with complicated installation, maintenance or daily routines. These unitary "blocks' will need to be designed to perform their tasks with the built-in features and no additional, extra cost additions required. We will specifically address the importance of designing devices that are also part of a differentiation strategy such as: product upselling/add-ons, horizontal/solution or vertical/segment strategies (see chapter 6).

- Low / no maintenance: IoT devices must have very low maintenance cycles and/or costs. IoT devices will be distributed with often reduced access, making replacement and maintenance costly and difficult.

- Connectivity & Security: IoT devices should be designed as de facto connected with graceful integration into the network and security transversal layers.

Manufacturers need to assess their willingness and overall strategic intent to enter this market or play in this layer. They need to be fast in their capability to deliver simple functions at a very low price with optimized delivery. On the other hand, the volume is going to be huge with high potential for profits.

Layer 2 - IoT Gateways

A high level of interoperability, redundancy, connectivity, pre-processing of data, aggregation of data, remote control and management leads to the requirement for gateways. These IoT gateways enable the connection of things, especially on the consumer front. They collect, elaborate, communicate and so forth. These will need to be affordable and at the same time fulfill the necessary requirements.

IoT Gateways need to be designed to handle devices and applications which use different protocols, standards and data formats. As time goes on, there will be a variety of different versions of each protocol, application, device, and anything else imaginable operating in the same environment at the same time.

Additionally, legacy machines, legacy protocols/buses sometimes decades old, will need to communicate with newer, more modern equipment and applications. The equipment, to unleash the data source, they represent will need to be connected in a cost and efficient way.

There is much effort put forth by multiple organizations to enable seamless connection of low power IoT endpoints, typically enabling an IoT Thing like a thermostat to run for a year on a button battery. However, regardless of the standard, IoT Things that make the jump from main power to running for months on batteries will need a gateway to provide:

- communication to the cloud and the IoT platforms
- specific applications / functions not delivered by the IoT Things endpoints
- protocol conversion
- local decision making
- local management and accessibility for users
- local pre-processed filtering and aggregation of data
- local additional processing power and storage
- local security

Layer 3 - IoT platforms

IoT platform's bundle many of the services needed that cannot be, for reasons of cost, redundancy, and scale, delivered by IoT gateways and IoT Things. IoT platform in the cloud as a service PaaS (platform as a service) will eventually be the chosen path as it enables answers to some of the IoT main roadblocks:

- Go to market
- Speed and costs of software developments
- Speed and costs of software deployment
- End-to-end security
- Customization
- Integration
- Scalability
- Flexibility
- Access-Anywhere Architecture

The most important value of IoT Platforms comes from the unleashed flow of data enabled by the IoT Devices and Gateways mixed with the integration of vertical applications, third party platforms and applications (analytics, business intelligence, etc.). It, in turn, enables analysis of the data and create the conditions for Artificial Intelligence making decisions based on it.

In an interview done by the author in July 2016 with Josef Brunner, CEO at Relayr, he stated that the big challenge for them was that IoT platforms are not about technologies but about use cases and end user benefits.

He considers that what is important is the integration of both ends of the downstream (meaning at the physical layer) and the upstream (meaning at the end user level) to deliver end use value. He added that the world is becoming more harmonized from a protocols perspective and that companies will lose their recurrent service revenues if they don't adapt and make the needed transformations and business model transitions.

He continued, saying that IoT transformation is about people and not technology. He stated: "we met with the Technology Officer from an analog company during a technology workshop. It was an all-day workshop, and after two hours, very politely but also very strictly, our investor stood up and said 'I don't think this is going anywhere, because you are still worrying about the technology and IoT has nothing to do with technology. We will solve every technology problem if we have to, but you have to make a business decision here in this company; either you are willing to change your business or we have to discontinue this discussion because in 5 years you're gone'. And that message was well received and they are now changing things from a senior leadership perspective, but they still have the legacy organization which they must keep on track while at the same time transforming."

One could consider that there will be the following types of IoT platforms delivering the following basic M2M services (74):

- Connectivity Support.
- Service Enablement.
- Device Management.
- Application Support.
- Solution Provider.

These expected services differentiate between IoT platforms and traditional M2M platforms. IoT platforms will have specific IoT capabilities such as Application development, Application management, Scalability as well as more traditional M2M platforms capabilities such as carrier and communications integrations, Device management and Operation environment (74).

We therefore expect the emergence of three types of platforms:

Connectivity platform:
The purpose of these platforms is to connect in a seamless and transparent way all possible IoT devices and gateways whatever the protocol and the associate connectivity. Similarly, to the Session Layer in

the OSI model, the platform provides services to establish connection between entities, to support orderly data exchange interactions, and to release the connection in an orderly manner (50) .Those platforms deliver a basic but value service which is global seamless connectivity which simplify the task of connecting and collecting data streams.

Integration platform or Application Enablement Platform (AEP):
An AEP is a form of platform-as-a-service meant to enable a developer to rapidly deploy an IoT application or service without worrying about scale-out or scale-up factor. As Luc Perard, head of EMEA IoT partner sales at Thingworx, writes in two LinkedIn posts (75) (76), a true, complete IoT "Application Enablement Platform" (AEP) is not just a "Device Cloud". It provides and abstracts all the foundational platform services so that enterprises can build their apps at a much higher level. This allows more people in the enterprise to participate in the development of apps while increasing the app development efficiency by an order of magnitude.

You would use an AEP to create:
- Vertical apps (= specific to a given use case or industry): Vertical IoT apps are well-known Some examples include telematics apps, smart city apps, connected health apps, remote industrial asset monitoring apps, etc.
- Horizontal apps (= applicable to multiple use cases or industries): Horizontal IoT apps are too often incorrectly labeled "platforms" by their creators. Some examples include device management apps, connectivity management apps. Per the definition above, these truly are just apps because they produce a result.

Business platforms and Applications (Vertical and Horizontal):
When addressing specific verticals such as smart "something" (smart hospitals, airports, etc.) there will be companies building applications above the IoT platforms (connectivity and AEP) or extending their current offers. These applications will also be fully leveraged by the digital channels such as system Integrators, general contractors, etc. The actual

services are provided by various businesses to service their customers using IoT. For example, a supermarket chain could offer services to connect smart refrigerators with their markets to make it easy for consumers to keep their food stocked and fresh.

Platforms will play a strategic role in the coming years as they are meant to be the meeting point between all major stakeholders willing to avoid the commoditization war of the lower layers. We have strong industrial players bringing to the market their deep industrial knowledge into their platforms. We also see brand new startups bringing to the market technology innovative IoT platforms with robust ecosystems. These would fall under the AEP with vertical and/or horizontal applications. At the same time, integrations platforms are beginning to emerge.

Numerous software players wanting the leverage the IoT trends, are beginning to rebrand their legacy, very often semi-proprietary, software platforms as IoT platform. But this will not last long as the need to have global, scalable and open platforms that deliver specific services (connectivity, integration and business applications) that will put the "rebranded" platforms under severe constraints.

Layer 4 - IoT User access and applications

This layer of IoT, as we are writing this book, is at the beginning of its evolution. Traditional operating systems (OSs) such as Windows and iOS were not designed for IoT applications. Google is beginning to accelerate in this space with Android Things: "Android Things is a turnkey solution that provides certified hardware to build IoT devices (77)" and Weave: "Weave is a communications platform for IoT devices that enables device setup, phone-to-device-to-cloud communication, and user interaction from mobile devices and the web (78)".

But this is just the beginning and we expect all major user access (HMI, OS, Hardware, etc.) to invest in the IOT space in the coming months and years as more and more connected things, associated platforms and applications are made available.

Layer 5 - IoT Network:

As stated earlier in this document, IoT is not a single system and is not defined by a common standard. Specific applications, usages, needs, network range, network topology, power source and throughput drives organizations to publish their own IoT "implementation" of those standards.

Even though the IoT Network layer will be made of different technologies, we believe that:

- Wireless networks will be a key component of the IoT network layer
- Software in the IoT network layer will take more and more importance as it holds a lot of value in the overall IoT value chain across the layers. We would not be surprised to see pure software players being attracted by this layer and pure networking players facing commoditization of their hardware and software.

IoT
WIRELESS
MARKET

**WHERE THE WIRELESS
THINGS ARE AND WHY**

40.2 % Business and Manufacturing
Real-time analytics of supply chains and
equipment, robotic machinery.

30.3 % Healthcare Portable
health monitoring, electronic recordkeeping,
pharmaceutical safeguards.

8.3 % Retail Inventory tracking
smartphone purchasing, anonymous analytics
of consumer choices.

7.7 % Security Biometrics and facial recognition locks,
remote sensors.

The overall
wireless chipsets
market revenue
in consumer
electronics
& automation
applications is expected
to reach **$20.4 billion** in 2017.

Wireless chipsets
market shipments
are expected to reach
4.86 billion
units in 2017.

Analog manufacturers often don't consider the network when designing their products. Instead, they need to understand the importance of the network layer, not just as a source of bandwidth, but as an enabler of value by providing enhanced stickiness between their products and the associated network.

There are numerous network topologies available that can be used when designing how IoT devices will connect with one another or will connect with gateways. I have illustrated some topologies on the next page to highlight the importance of choosing the most suitable IoT network topology to your use case. Some network topologies will be enablers for better connectivity, bandwidth, security in one use case while be a bottle neck on another use case.

Here are some network topologies:

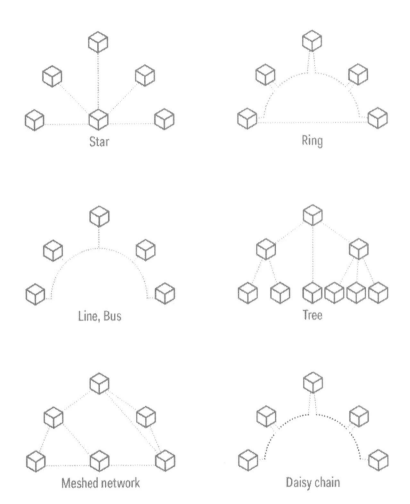

When designing IoT products or transforming an existing analog product portfolio, one must understand where the product or the range of products fits into this wireless network landscape. This is because connectivity will be one of the minimum requirements products will have to comply with and also because wireless networks enable far more flexibility than wired networks.

Unfortunately, the wireless landscape is made up of so many acronyms and protocols that it is necessary to clarify what are the most relevant and how to leverage those wireless protocols to transform and connect your current analog portfolio.

To begin classifying the most known technologies and protocols, we will use network range as a first filter. A network range is typically categorized into 5 classes:

- Proximity, body area networks – covers all wearable devices (including implants, surface mounted on the body, etc.)
- WPAN: Wireless Personal Area Network – covers a range of about 10 meters to 100 meters
- WLAN: Wireless Local Area Network – covers a range of about 100 meters to 1000 meters
- WNAN: Wireless Neighborhood Area Network – covers a range of about 1000 meters to 10 km
- WWAN: Wireless Wide Area Network – covers a range above 10km (as big as the entire globe of needed)

IoT WIRELESS TECHNOLOGIES

PROTOCOLS AND TECHNOLOGIES

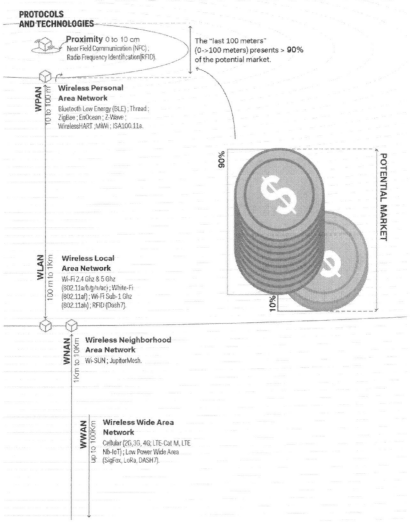

Proximity 0 to 10 cm
Near Field Communication (NFC) ;
Radio Frequency Identification(RFID).

The "last 100 meters"
(0->100 meters) presents > **90%**
of the potential market.

WPAN 10 to 100 m

Wireless Personal Area Network
Bluetooth Low Energy (BLE) ; Thread ;
ZigBee ; EnOcean ; Z-Wave ;
WirelessHART ;MiWi ; ISA100.11a.

90%

POTENTIAL MARKET

WLAN 100 m to 1Km

Wireless Local Area Network
Wi-Fi 2.4 Ghz & 5 Ghz
(802.11a/b/g/n/ac) ; White-Fi
(802.11af) ; Wi-Fi Sub-1 Ghz
(802.11ah) ; RFID (Dash7).

10%

WNAN 1Km to 10Km

Wireless Neighborhood Area Network
Wi-SUN ; JupiterMesh.

WWAN up to 100Km

Wireless Wide Area Network
Cellular (2G,3G, 4G; LTE-Cat M, LTE
Nb-IoT) ; Low Power Wide Area
(SigFox, LoRa, DASH7).

108

Transforming an analog offer portfolio into an IoT offer portfolio requires choosing very carefully which protocols you want to leverage and which applications you want to serve. Applications such as automotive, asset tracking, industrial networks, connected homes, smart grids and so forth require very different geographic coverage, network topologies and functionalities.

There is still an important fragmentation of the industry which in turn sees increasingly more Alliance/consortium types of organizations pushing for their own open stack/framework, which are very often proprietary, to get standardized and build an ecosystem of companies as part of their activity.

Below are descriptions of the key wireless technologies that appear to be leading the pack when looking at them from an IoT perspective (we will be using the network range as a filter):

Proximity Network

NFC (Near Field Communication)
NFC allows two-way indications between electronic devices, especially smart phones, to transfer digital contact information with applications such as contactless payment transactions, opening doors with secured NFC door locks, and connection to computers (79).

NFC has a range of less than 4 cm (80).

RFID (radio frequency identification)
RFID allows memorization and recovery of the digital information thru tags (active and passive) and tag readers. The main application of RFID technologies is for identification and tracking purposes (objects, animals, persons). There are different set of standards specific per industry and set by separate organizations such as the International Organization for Standardization (ISO), the International Electrotechnical Commission (IEC), the DASH7 Alliance and EPC global.

RFID passive tags have a typical range of about 1cm up to 5 meters; RFID active tags can reach up to 100 meters.

WPAN: Wireless Personal Area Network

Bluetooth

Bluetooth enables simple and low cost-efficient connections between mobile phones, smart things, and wearable products into small personal network, also called piconet. In the IoT space, Bluetooth technologies will typically be used to easily connect two devices that can deal with minimal configuration, and low speed such as thermostats, telephones, tablets, headsets, watches, and light switches.

The Bluetooth Special Interest Group (SIG) is the caretaker and creator of the core specification and service. There are mainly 2 types of Bluetooth: Bluetooth Basic Rate/Enhanced Data Rate (BR/EDR) for short-range continuous connection and Bluetooth with low energy (LE) for short bursts of long range connections. BLE uses IEEE 802.15.1. You will need different chips to leverage those implementations or chose dual-mode chipsets (81).

Bluetooth has a range between 1 cm up to 100 meters.

Thread

Thread is a recent royalty-free open standard protocol stack, introduced in 2014 by the "Thread Group" alliance (https://threadgroup.org/), and based on multiple standards which include IEEE802.15.4, IPv6 and 6LowPAN. It is reliable, cost-effective, low-power, wireless D2D (device-to-device) communication designed for Connected Home applications (82). The most interesting facts about Thread is that it supports mesh networks and can support up to two hundred and fifty nodes with authentication and encryption; also, it defines a portion of a typical IoT stack in a simple and quite elegant way. This will help IoT device manufacturers focus on their product rather than spending time on redefining IoT stacks.

Thread is becoming one of the most used stacks for the IoT for home automation in much the same way as the standard TCP/IP stack has been for the internet.

Thread Wireless range is about 120 feet or 40 meters. It can support up to 250 devices on a single meshed network.

Zigbee

ZigBee PRO (http://www.zigbee.org) from the ZigBee Alliance (consortium of manufacturers & developers) is a proprietary protocol stack using open standards. Its main objectives are to address low data-rates, low-power consumption meshed and star networks in particular commercial building automation and lighting control solutions. ZigBee PRO leverages the IEEE 802.15.4 (83).

Zigbee has a wireless range up to 70m indoors and 400m outdoors. It can support over 65,000 devices on a single network (84).

Z-Wave

Z-Wave is a wireless communications protocol for home automation and small commercial buildings mainly aimed for products which don't require a lot of power such as sensors and LEDs. Z-Wave leverages the IEEE 802.15.4 standard. The Z-Wave Alliance was established in early 2005 and groups more than 450 companies (85).

Wireless range of Z-Wave is about 120 feet or 40 meters. The maximum range with 4 hops is roughly 600 feet or 200 meters. It can support 255 devices on a single network (86).

EnOcean

EnOcean technologies are intended to leverage energy harvesting such as slight vibrations, temperature difference, and light in order to obtain self-powered wireless networks. The technology is typically used for home automation and commercial buildings. The technology has been ratified in 2012 by The International Electrotechnical Commission (IEC) (87).

EnOcean Wireless range is about 100 feet or 30 meters in buildings and can range up to 1000 feet or 300 meters outdoors.

WLAN: Wireless Local Area Network

Wi-Fi & Low Power Wifi - 802.11ah

Wi-Fi® leverages the Institute of Electrical and Electronics Engineers' (IEEE) 802.11 standards and is widely used because of its interoperability and also the fact that it can handle fast data transfer and large quantities of information. Wi-Fi Alliance® drives the adoption and evolution of Wi-Fi globally (88). Wi-Fi® is a trademark of the Wi-Fi Alliance®.

There are currently multiple protocols version in use such as 802.11a, 802.11g, 802.11n, etc.

Wi-Fi® will be a key component of the IoT network infrastructure due to the need to have fast wireless data transfer but has, unfortunately, a major disadvantage: it requires high power consumption which makes battery life in IoT devices a concern.

The Wi-Fi Alliance® introduced in 2016 an extension of Wi-Fi®: 802.11ah, also called Wi-Fi HaLow™, intended to answer to the specific needs of the IoT in, for example, connected homes, connected cars, Smart Cities: low energy and extended range (89).

Wireless range of Wi-Fi HaLow™ is expected to reach 1600 feet or 500 meters.

Dash7

DASH7 is based on the ISO 18000-7 Active RFID standard and is managed by the DASH7 Alliance similar to what the Wi-Fi Alliance® does for the Wi-Fi®. Dash7 is intended for building automation, connected homes, logistics, automotive, etc. It differentiates from Wi-Fi and Bluetooth by the fact that it provides longer range and has a very good behavior in indoors environments (90).

Dash7 is aiming at reaching between 300m and up to 1/5 km ranges. That range is much larger than the likes of ZigBee, but less than the maximum ranges quoted by Sigfox and LoRa.

WNAN: Wireless Neighborhood Area Network

Wi-SUN

Wi-SUN has the same objectives as other industry alliances such as the Wi-Fi Alliance® (who own the Wi-Fi trademark and leverages the IEEE 802.11 standard) or the WiMAX forum (who own the WiMAX trademark and leverages the IEEE 802.16 standard): be a certifying authority for interoperability testing focused on IEEE 802.15.4g and ipv6. IEEE 802.15.4g is an enhancement of the 802.15.4 towards large scale process control applications typically used in smart utilities networks (SUN) and smart grid networks (91).

JupiterMesh

JupiterMesh, also called ZigBee-NAN, is the intent of the ZigBee Alliance to expand beyond their short-range market. It's a mesh protocol using the 802.15.4g standard, as the Wi-SUN Alliance and was announced in June 2016 (92).

It is difficult to list all existing IoT "compatible" protocols as we consider the IoT being an evolution of the M2M market. There are multiple other wireless networking technologies such as ISA100.11a and WirelessHART for industrial applications for example.

WWAN: Wireless Wide Area Network

The WWAN is currently where the most important battle is taking place with very different strategic choices. We consider that, as we write this book, there are mainly 5 main technologies/approaches:

SigFox

Sigfox is both a network and a privately-owned company. Its aim is to become a global Internet of Things service provider (93). SigFox uses the Ultra Narrow Band (UNB) – sub GHz ISM band, which is a free frequency band. A Sigfox gateway can handle 1.3 million messages per 24 hours maximum, thus if each object transmits 10 messages per day this would be 130K objects. The network redundancy is achieved by overlapping cells coverage of 3 gateways. As the spectrum usage is not optimized this mean any message use the spectrum available to 3 gateways and thus its cell capacity is approximatively 130K / 3 = 43K objects/cell. A cell's range, in rural areas, is between 30 to 50 km and in urban areas between 3 to 10 km. The standby time for a 2.5 Ah battery with a SigFox access is about 20 years.

LoRa®

LoRaWAN ™ (Long Range Wide-area network) s an open global standard for wireless communication drive by the LPWAN industry through the LoRa Alliance™. The Alliance's aim is to provide both a standardized framework as well as it's associate technology hardware bricks that can be used by companies to guarantee interoperability (94); it has 500 members, covers over 50 nationwide deployments, 150 countries with smart city/enterprise networks and has over 100 LoRaWAN certified solutions. The LoRa Intellectual Property is owned by Semtech® who have invested around 300M$ in the technology and it is estimated some 100.000 developers are working on LoRa centric solutions. Semtech has licensed LoRa Intellectual Property to companies like Microchip and ST Microelectronics in order to ensure no single sourcing exists anywhere in the value chain. LoRa leverages the Ultra Narrow Band (UNB)-sub GHz ISM band which is free frequency bands. It's cell capacity is around 40,000 objects/cell and has a throughput of between 300 bps to 50 000 bps. The cell's range is, in rural areas, around 15 km and in urban areas, between 2 to 5 km. The stand by time for a 2.5Ah battery is about 20 years.

In an interview done by the author in November 2017 with Ir Jaap Groot, VP of Business Development at Semtech and Board Member of the LoRa Alliance, he stated that: "When you compare LoRA power consumption to cellular IoT technologies (LTE-M/NB IOT), LoRa is 5 to 10 times more power efficient in transmit and sleep, its peakpower (important for battery dimensioning and cost) is about 5 times lower than its cellular compagnons. One should position the cellular IoT and LoRa as complementary, hence many operators choose to deploy LoRa next to LTE-M. Important scalability for LoRa comes from the adaptive data rate, controlling the transmission speed (Kb/sec), which makes the networks infinitely scalable as the objects connect only to those gateways they need to (the higher the bitrate the lower the distance). A derived benefit is that LoRa can be deployed in very small gateways such as USB keys, set top boxes, routers and also Wifi hotspots. Other features include full bidirectional support, firmware or application updates over the air, geolocation without GPS and embedded security. On capacity the same argument as above, best measured by number of messages in uplink and downlink as objects differ in transmission frequency and the real limiting factor is time on air. However due to the adaptive data rate there is no limitation, when capacity is needed operators deploy new gateways, indoor, outdoor or even as USB keys in routers. Most important argument for cellular IoT versus LoRa is the fact one does not need licensed spectrum, hence the subscription can be a factor lower then cellular IOT and basically anyone can deploy a network.'"

Ingenu RPMA®

Ingenu is a privately-owned company that provides an entire stack for wireless networks based on their proprietary RPMA® (Random Phase Multiple Access) technology as well as a public network The Machine Network™ that can be used to sign up RPMA® enabled devices (96).

Ingenu leverages the Ultra Narrow Band (UNB)-2.4 GHz b which is a free frequency band. RPMA® cell capacity is around 500,000 objects/cell and has a throughput of about 625 000 bps. The cell's range is in urban areas around 15 km.

LTE-M, NB-lot and EC-GSM-loT

LTE-M, NB-lot and EC-GSM-loT are evolutions of existing mobile/cellular technologies for existing cellular network operators to leverage their existing geographic base stations' footprint, private radio spectrum (which ensures no coexistence issue with other cellular networks) and market access. EC-GSM-loT (Extended Coverage GSM for loT) is an improvement of GSM technologies due to the fact that GSM is still a dominant mobile technology in numerous markets. It also enables operators to extend the usage of their important 2G legacy installed base (97). eMTC (enhanced Machine Type Communication, often referred to as LTE-M) and NB-loT (Narrow Band Internet of Things) can be deployed together with legacy Long Term Evolution networks, or as stand-alone, in a reframed GSM carrier. They require a software upgrade of their existing network infrastructure (98).

Weightless

Weightless technology is being driven by the Weightless Special Interest Group (SIG). The SIG's objectives are to globalize the Weightless open standard as an alternative to short range loT wireless technologies as well as 3GPP technologies (EC-GSM-loT) and LTE based variants (LTE-M and NB-loT) (99).

There are different Weightless standards: Weightless-W, Weightless-N and Weightless-P.

Layer 6 - loT Security:

One of the largest and most important components of loT is security. Unfortunately, it is often an area that legacy analog companies are the least prepared to deal with, both in their products design as well as in their organizational setups. Lack of a coherent security mechanism in your future portfolio will lead to potential for attacks from a variety of sources including individual hackers, corporations committing espionage, and even cyber-warfare between nation states. Since it is estimated that within a decade there will be as many as a trillion devices accessing the Internet, security becomes paramount.

For example, high security is required for a smart home containing smart devices including solar power panels, security alarms, refrigerators, lightbulbs, and a television. On October 20th, 2016, a major cyberattack occurred against the U.S.-based internet domain host, Dyn. Part of this attack was carried out using internet-connected devices such as digital recorders and webcams, according to Dyn's chief strategy officer, Kyle York (100). About 100,000 Mirai IoT botnet nodes were used to attack at rates up to 1.2 Tbps (101). Stephanie Weagle, senior director at Corero Network Security, said the release of the Mirai code should be concerning for networking and security professionals worldwide, especially internet service providers (ISPs). She stated, "IoT devices are plug-and-play and the average user is incapable or uninterested in security and may never apply an upgrade or security patch to the device. So, if an IoT device ships with an exploitable vulnerability, it will likely remain vulnerable throughout its lifecycle.". This problem is exacerbated by the fact that most users will never change default usernames and passwords, said Weagle. "The bad guys know this and gain access to these devices in droves using well understood default credentials (102)".

IoT devices will be ubiquitous all over the planet, controlling more and more things, creating the conditions for major threats to countries, companies and individuals. The amount of damage that could potentially be done by malicious individuals or groups is phenomenal. One of the issues concerns the devices' security (login, passwords, physical interfaces and so forth) but also the fact that there is an ever-increasing amount of protocols needed to deal with applications and wireless networks, creating the need to have important protocols colocation in gateways and platforms which, by design, creates security holes.

An IoT device will need to be uniquely identified, whether it be a smart house, smart factory, or even a single air pressure sensor mounted on the roof of a home. This introduces a whole new level of complexity and security that must be part, as earlier as possible, of the offer creation process for IoT compatible products and systems. IoT devices will be moved, repaired, modified or swapped out on a regular basis and must therefore be designed accordingly.

Connected devices and the associate IoT components such as gateways, platforms and so forth generate vast amounts of data, even when considering only the information from a single person. That data includes payments, medical information, GPS travel information, and even every word spoken and every sound made in a household. All this information is often stored in the cloud for personal use but also as a source of information for more advanced analytics.

The data challenge
The vast amount of data that is available from IoT and other digital methods is valuable in its own right as a business asset. This data and the resultant analysis can be used by businesses to monitor and provide guidance for changes in the services and products they offer, as well is in the way businesses operate.

There are technical challenges in gathering this volume of data:

First and foremost, real-time transmission of information from devices such as sensors can require far more bandwidth than is available. Consider, for example, a smart operating room in the hospital, which could contain a wide variety of sensing devices to monitor every aspect of a patient's health including their breathing, heart rate, blood levels, and even skin color and muscle tone. This is an overwhelming amount of information and to provide good patient care, it must be analyzed in real time. Doing so allows very quick decisions to be made, perhaps even automatically, to improve patient health and the possibility of survival.

The second is the aggregation and intelligence that can be extracted from it. Aggregating all the data so that it can be useful presents another challenge. When considering the concept of smart homes scattered throughout a major metropolitan area, the amount of data is immense and continuous. This information is also extraordinarily useful when examined on an aggregate level. Doing so, you could predict resource usage throughout the city by analyzing the aggregate data and then factoring in the effects of the weather, social events, and other variables. Let's take the example of a smart stadium that was connected to the surrounding metropolitan area. In a large event, such as a football game, it's predictable that there will be a surge of traffic as the event begins and ends. Sensors could report on the number of people in the stadium, and adjust traffic patterns automatically as those people begin to leave the parking area. Businesses in the local area – such as restaurants – which normally close early, could receive notifications of the traffic surge and remain open longer.

The third challenge is the storage and legal ownership of the data. Does the customer own their information? Or do the companies and businesses which collect information own it? Or perhaps the data aggregators own the data; or is the data, once personalized information has been removed, available to the public domain? There is also the legal aspect of it: today's laws might need to be adapted to cope with global connected things generating more data on private information than any other system/software has in the recent years.

Smart and connected power grids
Internet of things will definitely change the way power is consumed and produced and distributed. End to end connectivity on power grids has never been deployed; connecting demand and generation, unleashing the data that this connection enables will have important impacts on the way our society operates. We should not underestimate the societal benefits of such connected grids which brings to the final customer far more information on the direct impact between individual behaviors and the associate carbon footprints.

There will also be more and more alternative and distributed sources of energy, which in turn, will raise the complexity of such connected grids. When looking back at what network infrastructure looked like in the 90's, and how it evolved in 10 years moving from basic hub to fully routed/intelligent networks, is a good indicator of what power grid will be going through in the next 10 to 15 years. Digitization of the energy industry, distributed power sources, storage and intelligent grid will have similar impacts, if not greater, than what the internet had on the way we live our everyday life.

Power grids are at the core of our world's functionality. A country can operate without petrol, but would struggle without power. Petrol, nuclear plants, water dams are, for example, means to get power. Computers, smartphones, for example are means to get information. Who controls information and power can greatly impact our societies and countries.

IoT will be a game changer for this industry and the associate ecosystem. Asset performance management will typically benefit from such changes in the way energy is consumed. We will see more and more real-time supply and demand platforms emerge which will have a direct impact on energy storage, network control and management and so forth. Utilities will also be highly impacted. As stated in IoT and the Future of Networked Energy, A Platform for Enhanced Energy Cloud Applications, Services, and Business Models, written by Neil Strother - Principal Research Analyst and Mackinnon Lawrence - Senior Research Director Published 4Q 2016 by the Navigant Research: "a utility that can delay or avoid investing another $2 billion in generation plants and delivery systems by assembling a smarter IoT-enabled grid is a stronger player. Alternatively, an IoT investment of $2 billion would build the foundation needed to compete for the $1.3 trillion in annual new revenue that will be created across the Energy Cloud in 2030 (103)".

The benefits of getting not only the power demand but also the power generation connected are immense; but the associate risks are even greater. All networks can be hacked, it's just a matter of time and means. Will power grids be hacked? Yes, however that is not the right question. It is: 'who and which organization will hack the grid?', and 'What are the risk mitigation plans and systems to be deployed when this happens?'. Power is the blood of our economies. Securing the grid, the end to end connection will be an important challenge in the coming years, not only for the utilities but for all the stakeholders in the power generation and consumption value chain.

Why Blockchain might be the answer
Blockchain technology promises to be the missing link enabling peer to peer contractual behavior without any third party to "certify" the IoT transaction. It also answers the challenge of scalability, single point of failure, time stamping, record, privacy, trust and reliability in a very consistent way.

Blockchain technology could provide a simple infrastructure for two devices to directly transfer a piece of property (ex: money, data, etc.) between one another with a secured and reliable time-stamped contractual handshake. To enable message exchanges, IoT devices will leverage smart contracts which then model the agreement between the two parties. This feature enables the autonomous functioning of smart devices without the need for centralized authority. If you then extend this peer-to-peer transaction to human to human or human to objects/platforms, you end up with a fully distributed trustworthy digital infrastructure.

Blockchain promises to be a key accelerator of the IoT evolution and spread among all industries and usages as it solves the major roadblock of the IoT: trust, ownership and record. The technology will disrupt not only banking ecosystem and associate financial transactions, but will open the door to a series of IoT usages/applications that will create tomorrow's unicorns.

SUMMARY

By its very nature, the Internet of things will bring massive amounts of change in the market which in turn will introduce challenges for businesses and manufacturers. It is vital that companies maintain the ability to recognize, when applicable, that their business models will need to adjust, determine what needs to be done, and quickly modify the way they operate in a lesser or greater degree. Some of these changes may be so significant as to require a complete pivot of the analog business into the digital world.

Digital transformation can drive financial performance on one side if properly tackled but can, as well, need so many adjustments that it may put the core business of a company at stake.

Technology providers such as manufacturers, software companies, and System Integrators, will be required to change their mindset and receive specialized training to become and remain highly skilled at installing both software and hardware, customizing IoT applications, integrating large number of devices so they operate together in harmony, troubleshooting, and supporting and managing the IoT environment.

The common denominator is that to leverage IoT requires that businesses be willing and able to "pivot hard," changing direction as required due to changes in technology, communications, and customer desires and requirements.

On one side, you have IoT technologies and standards that are diverse and doomed to evolve on a regular basis; on the other side, analog companies willing to pivot hard and make their analog product offering more IoT enabled while at the same time not falling into the commoditization space.

Summary: The IoT^4 strategic methodology leverages the 6 layers of architecture highlighted in this chapter. This is what we call the first step of the methodology which helps to move an existing analog portfolio into an IoT compatible offer using this leveraging power.

STEP 1
Making your analog portfolio
IoT compatible

Unbundle and map your current product and software
portfolio into an IoT compatible offering using
the 6 IoT layers.

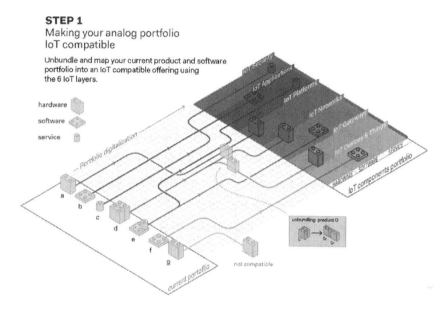

CHAPTER 6

IOT^4 METHODOLOGY
STEP 2:
DEFINING OFFERING DIFFERENTIATION
STRATEGIES

"Technology... is a queer thing. It brings you great gifts with one hand, and it stabs you in the back with the other."
Carrie Snow

As part of the IoT[4] strategic methodology, we will be discussing the second step: Offering differentiation strategies. This will demonstrate how well established analog companies can leverage their core offer, compatible with the IoT (see step 1, described in the previous chapter), to avoid commoditization.

IS IOT YOUR BIGGEST THREAT OR YOUR LARGEST OPPORTUNITY?

Let us focus some time on the classic example that represents how digital transformation can challenge an existing model and how it can harm and threaten the existence of a well-established leader. Kodak® is this excellent example. Most people believe they missed a technology shift when instead, there were deeper foundational cracks that led to the slow disintegration of their business model.

The root causes of this industrial and social disaster are outlined below:

- R & D: Did they simply not invest enough into it? No. Kodak invented the technology and aggressively invested up to $2 Billion in R&D for digital imaging (104). Semiconductor technologies without a doubt already formed Kodak's core knowledge and potential niche market; but they did realize as management was tracking the rate of which digital cameras replaced traditional film cameras.
- Leadership: Was it a lack of leadership that became blindsided? No. In 1996, CEO George Fisher knew that digital photography could highly disturb, or even replace Kodak's core business. The leadership was in fact, aware of the threat that digitization was bringing (105).
- Acquisitions: Was Kodak focused on internally developing all relevant technologies without looking at acquiring external startups to help with the digital shift? No. Kodak acquired Ofoto in 2001 and renamed it "Kodak EasyShare Gallery" in 2005. The site was Kodak's consumer online digital photography web site. Ofoto was started in 1999. This

acquisition proves that Kodak not only had identified the threat and the associated opportunities but had also executed a plan to leverage the digital transformation of their market.

Kodak's bad strategic and investment timing

Chunka Mui , in his "How Kodak Failed" article published on January 18th, 2012 on Forbes (106) highlights the following: Barabba (head of market intelligence in 1981) had done a deep dive on the future adoption curves from the analog silver halide films versus the digital photography. He highlighted the fact that digital photography could possibly replace Kodak's analog base business but also and importantly, that this would not happen overnight and consequently the company had around 10 years to strategize and execute a digital transformation. Barabba sheds light on the fact that executive management was so worried about the digital photography threat, that they executed a strategy based on digital kiosks (10,000). Unfortunately, the team did not realize that the digital photography market would evolve towards home storage and home printing capabilities, and not remain dependent on photography services in these areas.

This example shows that the first ones to enter carry an important portion of the risks implied by testing unproven business models and carrying the R&D costs resulting from multiple available technologies that have not yet proven their relevancy. It also shows the importance of strategic timing that we will deep dive into in the following "false belief" paragraph (106).

Kodak remained complacent in their analog success and acted like a stereotypical change-resistant organization

Kodak applied their well-established analog business references (product, margin split, product performance and specification, price points, channels: Kodak digital kiosks) and this later proved difficult to change. Kodak tried to simplify and adapt to technologies, but as illustrated in the example of digital kiosks, doing something and doing the right thing are different things.

Important contrast to Kodak's failure is Fujifilm's successful shift.

In his blog entry "How Fujifilm survived" (107), KNC, the economist explains that Fujifilm realized in the 80s that digital photography was going to be the next big transformation they would face. The executive management, mainly from the very profitable film division, took the decision to milk the analog cow. The slow analog film business fall took 15 to 20 years and went from 60% of Fujifilm's profits to basically nothing. Kodak and Fujifilm both had quickly identified the trends and possible impact to their profitability. So why was the result so different between the two leaders? Kodak nearly disappeared and Fujifilm leveraged this transformation to leap in front of its competitors?

KNC highlights the main difference between these two competing companies when dealing with digital transformation:

- Strategy and Execution: Fujifilm management decided to diversify and adopt a long-term vision that enabled them to sacrifice some short-term profitability to harvest long term gains. Fujifilm also understood the importance of expertise and key digital skills as part of its workforce.
- Self-cannibalization: Fujifilm understood that the analog film and digital film market were serving a similar application and usage. The market transforms according to the evolutions of technologies. Fujifilm that had a strong market position did not hesitate to cannibalize its own space to enable long term success.

Kodak's leadership failed to manage simultaneously competitive frames and business models.

The main mistakes and root causes have been very well explained by Clark Gilbert and Joseph L. Bower in their article "Disruptive Change: When Trying Harder Is Part of the Problem" published in the Harvard Business Review from the original Kodak case study done in May 2002, concluded that Kodak had fallen into the trap of trying to make the new digital business model fit their old, but very successful, analog model instead of figuring out the best model in order to serve new needs and applications.

In the same article, there is a very good assessment of digital transformation and innovation as a threat or as an opportunity:

- Threat: When the disruptive innovations begin to be identified, the most efficient option is to frame them as a threat, to properly allocate the right resources and funding. It will also drive the proper behavior from the organization and will push the managers to focus their efforts to deal with the needed transformations.
- Opportunity: On the opposite end, when creating a new business model and assessing the market on new services, usages and applications, it is more efficient to frame those disruptive innovations as an opportunity. This will in turn trigger the proper behavior from the organization to find unique applications associated with the identified disruptions.

The authors also highlight that managing competing threat and opportunity frames at the same time often equates to adjustments to organizational structure and the processes governing new business funding and that this is the key to an effective response (105).

Fujifilm's strategic approach was so dramatically different than Kodak's: Fujifilm's executive management understood that the long-term success of the company was tightly linked to the capability of the organization to manage the two competing frames.

What about mature and early stage companies: do they value digital transformation as a threat or an opportunity? The MITSloan Management review (108) shows that maturing company respondents overwhelmingly view digital technologies as an opportunity (around 95%) more than a threat (around 28%). On the other side, early stage companies have tendencies to reduce the gap between opportunity and threat; they view digital technologies as much as an opportunity (around 40%) as a threat (around 30%).

IoT therefore needs to be treated as both a threat and an opportunity but not for the same reasons. The difference is how your company, your leaders and middle management address it and implement the right business models with the proper commitment of resources and allocation. The rules of the game are changing for numerous markets once considered as "stable" with well-established analog leaders. Thus, you need to assess if this is applicable to your market, and if your answer is "maybe" then you need to frame it in the most efficient way to gain long term success.

FALSE BELIEF: YOU NEED TO BE THE FIRST ONE TO SUCCEED

There is a common belief that first in are always the winners, that to leverage digital transformation and innovation the first is the one that takes it all. Bill Gross, IdeaLab's CEO, did a research study (109) (available on http://www.idealab.com) on what made start-ups successful amongst 5 essential elements: ideas, team, business model, funding and finally timing. The results show that timing is, by 42%, the number one success factor across more than 200 companies.

Innovation enables pioneers to defend their market share against new entrants. Peter N. Golder and Gerard J. Tellis, in their research *Pioneer Advantage: Marketing Logic or Marketing Legend* (31) highlight that market pioneers are, de facto, market leaders upon entry. However this leadership does not appear to last very long (12 years on average) before being leap frogged by later entrants.

Their results suggest that "being first in a new market may not confer automatic long-term rewards. An alternative strategy worth considering may be to let other firms pioneer and explore markets, and enter after learning more about the structure and dynamics of the market. Indeed, early leaders who entered an average of 13 years after the pioneer are more likely than pioneers to lead the market today (31)".

Kodak is a perfect example, as pioneers on one side of the coin, and late bloomers, on the other. They were pioneers with regard to their early investment into digital kiosks. However, their flawed strategy and lack of prompt action, in general made them late comers without a plan.

FALSE BELIEF: YOU NEED TO BE A DIGITAL STARTUP TO SUCCEED

Another common belief is that start-ups have all the cards in their hands to beat the well-established analog companies. In fact, analog companies have great weapons to fight back and even lead the digital transformation; especially if they leverage their considerable resources to fight off the attacks including:

- Investment capitals
- Production capabilities
- Strong brands & demand generation
- Strong channels
- In depth relationships with global accounts
- Sales force on the ground
- Influence power: Standardization, market price, specifiers, etc.

When you add those two elements – time and assets - it's not too late for incumbents/analog companies to adapt; they in fact have what is needed to lead and beat competition leveraging and adapting to the new rules of the game.

OFFERING DIFFERENTIATION STRATEGIES-TRANSFORMATION FROM THE EDGE:

As highlighted in the previous paragraphs, it is important to understand the possible changes that may occur, to assess the level of risk these changes might have for your core analog business and elaborate a strategy that leverages not only your current resources but also your competitors' weaknesses.

Once leaders share a common understanding of the situation, of the threat and the opportunity that the IoT brings to the table, there are key strategic paths that need to be reviewed and a direction to be chosen. As stated previously in this book, there are 4 possible strategies or scenarios for an analog company when dealing with digital transformation:

- Ignore
- Milk the cow
- Transforming from the edge
- Put it off

There are no right or wrong options. It's a matter of where the market you operate in is moving, what position you have in this market, the ecosystem and channels you rely on to build your value proposition and your strategic timing.

Even though companies need to go through digital transformation, it is vital that they keep the everyday operations (what we call the "analog mothership") working in the markets where they make their money.

What we address primarily in this book is how analog companies can prepare for what might happen, the different options when facing digital transformation, within the field of the IoT, with all its specific implications. It may not be necessary to change the mothership, or possibly it may need to be completely rebuilt from the ground up.

The next question is what does it mean from a practical perspective? What needs to be highlighted as an extension of the core of the enterprise to accomplish success in leveraging what the IoT brings to the table? What type of edging are accessible when talking about the IoT?

Alan LEWIS and Dan McKONE in their 2016 book: *Edge strategy™: A New Mindset for Profitable Growth* (110) have highlighted the importance of leveraging more of the existing assets and investments to:

- harvest more value from existing assets and therefore raise profit margin.
- lower investment risks.
- expand the customer reach by answering to more needs.
- raise customer satisfaction.

If you are an analog company looking for opportunities to leverage the IoT transformation through a "transformation from the edge" strategy, then you will need to consider it through 3 types highlighted by Alan LEWIS and Dan McKONE (111):

- Product Edge: This type is about providing an 'extra' to some customers to fit their needs and their willingness to pay for it. Calibration of a product (we can consider, to a certain extent, that a service is also a product) is about maximizing revenue based on the value added of the basic product as well as the available upsell triggered by add-ons/extensions.
- Journey Edge: This type is about providing a better overall customer experience and journey by specifically answering the customers' needs and final objectives. This is triggered by an expansion, bundling of existing products and services to improve the customer's experience.
- Enterprise Edge: This type is about leveraging existing assets such as products, services, real estate but also non-tangible assets such as data that already exist in the company to repackage them according to specific customer business needs.

APPLYING THE EDGE STRATEGY™ CONCEPT TO THE IOT:

By applying the Edge Strategy™ (Product, Journey and Enterprise) to the IoT, you will understand the moves you need to make and the technology layers that affect your core offer and achieve enormous success:

	Edge Strategy™: beating the commoditization cycle	IoT4 strategy: Defining an offering differentiation strategy to avoid commoditization
Strategy N°1	"Edge of the product" "Edge-based customization"	Product upselling / add-ons move
Strategy N°2	"Edge-based bundling"	Horizontal / solution move
Strategy N°3	"Edge-based solutions"	Vertical / segment move

Here are the descriptions of those different moves:

Product upselling / Add-ons move

Core IoT compliant (with standards, non-custom based functions) bricks will face commoditization. These will be similar in concept to Lego™ or LittleBits™ bricks: standard color, standard size, standard function, and standard connectivity.

This option is truly about how to move your Core IoT components or bricks into a space where customers will be willing to pay more to get a small but valuable extra that could answer to their specific needs. These "smaller extras" can be hardware components, software add-ons, or services.

You might realize that you could charge the "extra something" instead of giving it away as part of a package. This identifies another challenge of this move: how to determine what is the minimum viable product verses extra cost add-ons. The minimum viable product (MVP™) defined by Frank Robinson, CEO, SyncDev, Inc, is a product that has just those core features sufficient to deploy the product and no more, which in turn means that functions, or smaller extras, are not needed as part of the MVP and therefore can be charged back as value added to the basic product, to the reseller and/or end user (112).

We call this move the Product Upselling/Add-ons Move.

Horizontal / Solution Move

This move or option is about how to move or bundle some of your Core IoT components brick into a space where customers will be willing to pay more to get a solution across one or several layers of the IoT architecture. The Edge Strategy™ refers to an "Edge-based bundling"; we consider that, in the IoT, the Edge-based approach is how analog manufacturers bundle their products and services to better address needs and end-user experience.

IoT customers will be willing to pay more for the simple, already tested, integration (hardware, software and/or services) to enhance and improve their overall journey. Companies willing to make this move understand their customers' needs and can leverage some of their bricks and develop a horizontal bundle with third parties to deliver this peace of mind to customers. These third parties can be hardware, software and service providers but also a developer's community willing to deliver more through an integration horizontal.

We call this the Solution Horizontal move.

Vertical / Segment Move

This move or option deals with how to propose a full end-to-end unique bundle to customers ready to pay for fully integrated systems and solutions. Some customers require systems that are designed for their vertical markets and customized for their specific needs. Because the IoT will be very open, by building on what we call Lego components and bricks, there will be space for those vertical, end to end, IoT systems. The Vertical IoT move answers to specific Service Level Agreements, for integration from end to end with third parties.

Companies wanting to make this move will need to have a deep understanding of their customers' culture, market and setting in which the solution will be deployed. The Oil and Gas and healthcare markets are perfect examples.

This move is the most complex, costly and time consuming. Over time we expect to see more and more players wanting to fill up this space and packaged vertical solutions with large-scale horizontal platforms taking hold.

We call this the Solution Vertical/Segment move.

Summary: The second step of the methodology represents all the different available options for existing analog companies to leverage their current analog core offering as well as their IoT compatible portfolio (hardware, software, and services) to avoid commoditization.

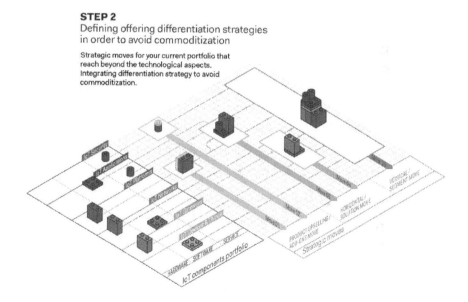

STEP 2
Defining offering differentiation strategies
in order to avoid commoditization

Strategic moves for your current portfolio that
reach beyond the technological aspects.
Integrating differentiation strategy to avoid
commoditization.

CHAPTER 7

IOT⁴ METHODOLOGY
STEP 3:
CHOOSING THE MOST RELEVANT BUSINESS
MODELS

"If you went to bed last night as an industrial company, you're going to wake up this morning as a software and analytics company".
Jeff Immelt, CEO General Electric

Choosing the most relevant business model is only feasible when you have enough clarity on how you will make your analog portfolio "compatible" as well as a defined differentiation strategy to avoid commoditization.

Business models are as important as a strong offer portfolio as well as a value based market positioning.

As previously shared, we expect to see the rise of three possible offering differentiation strategies. These are:

- Product upselling/Add-ons move
- Horizontal/Solution move
- Vertical/Segment move

If you apply to those the 2 possible financial models: OPEX or CAPEX based, you end up with 6 possible business models:

IoT offering	Business categories	
	CAPEX	OPEX
Product upselling / add-ons Move	Product edge Transactional upselling: Software add-ons, Physical add-ons	Product upselling / add-ons move Recurrent upselling: Software add-ons – licensing. Product, platforms, application sold as a service. Physical add-ons – Leasing. Subscriptions: maintenance/warranty/Service attached to product
Horizontal / Solution Move	Journey edge Transactional Horizontal / Solution upselling: Packaging systems and sold as one-off	Horizontal / solution move Recurrent Horizontal / Solution upselling: bundling product together. System and solution as a service)
Vertical / Segment Move	Enterprise edge Transactional Vertical / Segment upselling: fully integrated System and solution sold as one-off	Vertical / segment move Recurrent Vertical / Segment upselling: fully integrated System and solution sold as a service. Performance: Service level agreements sold as a service or as a lease

BUSINESS
MODELS

The IoT will support total services spending of
$ 235 billion in 2016 according to Gartner estimate.

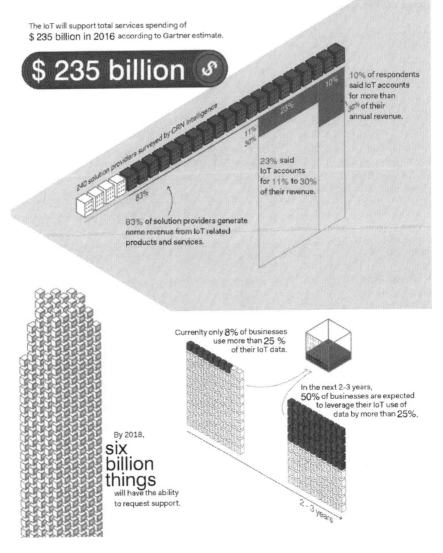

$ 235 billion

240 solution providers surveyed by CRN Intelligence

83%

10% of respondents
said IoT accounts
for more than
30% of their
annual revenue.

23% said
IoT accounts
for 11% to 30%
of their revenue.

83% of solution providers generate
some revenue from IoT related
products and services.

Currenlty only 8% of businesses
use more than 25 %
of their IoT data.

In the next 2-3 years,
50% of businesses are expected
to leverage their IoT use of
data by more than 25%.

By 2018,
**six
billion
things**
will have the ability
to request support.

2 - 3 years

142

There are two possible business categories and three IoT strategic models for each one. These are discussed below:

ONE-OFF - CAPEX MODELS:

- Transactional upselling: Software add-ons, Physical add-ons
- Transactional Horizontal / Solution upselling: Packaging systems and sold as one-off
- Transactional Vertical / Segment upselling: fully integrated System and solution sold as one-off

RECURRENT - OPEX MODELS

- Recurrent upselling: Software add-ons – licensing. Product, platforms, and applications sold as a service. Physical add-ons – Leasing. Subscriptions: Maintenance/Warranty/Service attached to product
- Recurrent Horizontal / Solution upselling: bundling product together, system and solution as a service)
- Recurrent Vertical / Segment upselling: fully integrated System and solution sold as a service. Performance, Service level agreements sold as a service or as a lease

STEP 3
Choosing the most relevant business models

Map of where different strategic moves fit in the 5 layers of architecture and which financial model fits best.

In this chapter, we address each one of those business models so to explain what it means when used with an analog core offering.

CAPEX MODELS:

Capex is the one-off model which means that the money is earned at the time of sale. This is the traditional product sales model. These types of models can be very valuable for players positioning themselves as providers of basic hardware and software components as they will catch the value once: at the point of sale with no recurring option to extend their value proposal forward through time (catching at the same time the recurrent revenue).

One-off -Transactional upselling

If we are considering the following:

- That the IoT will build itself up as basic, interchangeable and compatible basic components.
- that IoT will at one point standardize itself to leverage high volume and scale approaches to those unitary components.
- that the share of value overtime of both basic hardware and associated software will decline.

If all three of these are true, then the players willing to leverage the CAPEX business models will need to understand which technology basic components can be generalized for both: standalone components and components as part of a system and a solution.

We expect that the Capex models will be driven mainly by high volume of basic unitary components companies. Upselling in this model is done through providing basic features (software and/or hardware) which value brought is higher than the cost of sell.

The companies choosing this edging strategy will face commoditization. The only way for them to thrive will be to influence standards, master the 'go to market' timing and leverage their Intellectual property / patents in order to propose unique technologies and achieve mass adoption.

Upselling in this model is accomplished by providing basic feature Minimum Valuable Products.

One-off -Transactional Horizontal / Solution upselling or Solution Bundling Upselling

Packaging basic components (hardware, software, and services) into a system and selling it as one-off is one of the capex edging strategies.

Mixing end devices across the different IoT layers such as sensors, actuators and gateways but also across the same layers such as multiple sensors to sell specific value to end users and/or channels such as performance, specific applications / features, ease of installation is a typical approach of such upselling technique.

One of the challenges of this edging strategy, when dealing with an open and interoperable market, is with the value needed to fill the gap between standardization and end users' usages/needs. The more the IoT standardizes and enables high interoperability at a reasonable cost, the more will the IoT platforms embrace specific applications and features.

One-off -Transactional Vertical / Segment upselling

The need for fully integrated systems to deliver specific performance, service level and/or end to end customization will drive the expansion of this upselling model.

This edging strategy responds to the following paradigm that the IoT will trigger. The IoT will push for the need for low cost / interoperable unitary components, but at the same the team will need to answer the requirements of specific segments and/or users to have IoT systems tailor made / end to end, that embraces hardware, software, installation, and the integration of third party hardware and software.

The ability of companies to provide those end-to-end systems which answer and embrace specific segments needs, processes, and ecosystems will enable them to establish deep and long-term commercial relationships with those specific end-users.

As the IoT landscape matures over time, you will see integrated segment IoT leaders. The value brought not only by filling the gap between layers, but more importantly by delivering specific end to end performance, features, and integration for specific use will be recognized.

Companies choosing this edging model will not face commoditization as they will be able to design segment-specific, with built in customization options, IoT systems at a price that end users are willing to pay for that particular extra result, performance and feature set.

One-off vertical upselling is not the best option as you carry the burden of an end to end system without the recurrent monetary reward. Even upselling from a one-off perspective is a difficult move. This move is interesting if you have very specific components in the IoT layers such as explosion-proof end devices for oil industries or germ-free gateways for hospitals that are needed by end-users, which are willing to pay this extra money to get the added performance.

RECURRENT - OPEX MODELS:

IoT unleashes data that was once inaccessible which enables real time flow of information. This stream of information then helps to create knowledge, added value services (on and off site) improving the overall performance and reducing downtime. This is just an example of what the IoT will enable. The move from a product sale to a service sale and from a one-off sale to an as-a-service sale will be the direction most companies will try to move their business.

An "as-a-service" sale embraces not only the access to the asset that could be rented with the installation and maintenance, but also the access to the flow of data and associated software services such as the analytics built above it.

Analog manufacturers that once sold a product with very low recurrent revenue stream but that holds a lot of embedded value/information, can leverage the IoT to unleash this value and develop disruptive business models to leap frog their competitors.

For IoT suppliers, the Opex model does bring challenges to the floor such as the usage of capital needed to build all necessary platforms, infrastructure and absorb all associated costs of customization, deployment and maintenance.

The "as a service" model is highly valued not only by end users to avoid capital utilization but also by chief financial officers as it enables a steady and predictable flow of revenue.

If you are wondering which edging strategy fits well to beat commoditization, Recurrent model is a good choice. Connecting devices to each other and to the cloud allows you to create a recurrent flow of revenue, and to sell additional products and services to give even more functions to the consumer.

Connecting your customers and unleashing their data should be a priority of any analog company wanting to drive recurrent revenue streams. You can use the vast amount of data collected from their IoT devices and stored in the cloud to provide additional services and analytics. This data can also be used to drive upsells and offer even more services that they can purchase on a recurring basis.

Recurrent upselling
Software add-ons and licensing features that were once embedded as part of your basic offerings is a typical recurrent upselling. Product software upgrades driven by the needs of having up-to-date, cyber-secured platforms is another way to leverage this recurrent model.

Renting access to online applications as a recurrent service is an elegant method to avoid one-off software sales and at the same time raise customer's satisfaction to the ease of use (no hardware, software upgrades, onsite maintenance, costs of costly servers to run the applications and associated databases, integrity of data, etc.). This means converting your product sales into a recurrent fee model, as if you were renting a car. Both Adobe with their Creative Cloud offering and Microsoft with the Office 365 products are good examples of this model.

Finally, subscription fees attached to a physical product such as maintenance/warranty/Service can transform a one-off sale into a recurrent stream of revenue.

Recurrent Horizontal / Solution upselling

The horizontal model applies mainly to the consumer market, although there are applications in the business world as well. In this an IoT enabled gateway allows various devices to interoperate and share data to give the consumer higher service.

High customization of the environment is a core value of horizontal approach. Driving recurrent revenue through software enhancement (add-ons) of standard hardware and software components of a horizontal system/solution, is a typical recurrent horizontal upselling move.

Let's take the example of a home equipped with several IoT smart devices: a refrigerator, sensors outdoors and indoors, an alarm system and a connection to the so-called smart electrical grid and water services.

The alarm system can build up a history of who has accessed the home to gain a clear picture of people authorized for entry. Thus, the homeowner, family and a few close friends may be granted access without needing keys or passwords. If the alarm system noted a consistent pattern of a family member or friend not to allowed access, then it could automatically deny entrance, even with a password or keys, if the owner was absent.

In addition, the alarm system would be able to command the lights throughout the home. If it detects a possible intruder, lights could be turned on in an appropriate pattern (instead of randomly) to give the appearance that someone is at home.

External sensors can keep track of the weather and temperature outside. These will communicate with the smart electrical grid to inform it of the need for increased power usage for the air conditioning. In turn, the grid can communicate back to the home if there are power shortages and will prevent appliances such as laundry services from being used at those times.

The smart refrigerator, being informed of the heat outside, will speed up the ice making service and ensure there is plenty of cold water available. It could also order additional supplies directly from Amazon or the local supermarket to prepare for the heat wave.

None of these responses need to be programmed directly into these smart devices, since they would build up a history over time, and learn which actions they need to take to provide optimum service to the consumers in the house. The smart grid and water services will build up the same kind of historical understandings.

The point of these examples is to demonstrate that IoT devices are extremely valuable to consumers as a system or a solution but also if they add customization value to the end user. If you extend this and add historical data, connectivity and enhancement of this horizontal system with cloud based applications such as analytics and virtual intelligence, then the value is multiplied many times over.

Recurrent horizontal solution upselling is the capability to bundle a set of products and services together and to charge a recurring fee for access to those services and any add-on service.

When designing your offerings and marketing programs to leverage the value of this inter-communication, it is important to tackle both the Capex and Opex sides. These devices will generate data; the long term value is in the data and the associated enhancement it enables.

The value is in the data and the associated enhancement.

An excellent example of the horizontal model is the Apple Homekit™. This application supports hundreds of compatible devices, tying them all together in an interoperable system that can be controlled from a Smartphone. Apple is well known not only because of its innovative product and SKUs but also through the developers' community which has built the software add-ons that iTunes and the Apple store bring to their products. Apple's success is due not only to the recurrent upselling model pertaining to its own products, but also for that which benefits their community.

Recurrent Vertical / Segment upselling

The vertical model primarily applies to businesses that need tighter controls, have regulatory oversight, or have needs which supports large numbers of customers, clients and suppliers. Examples include oil refineries, hospitals, water districts, mining, agriculture and other industries.

An example of a vertical market is the data center. In this case, it is very important to maintain excellent environmental control, high-availability, and good performance. In the past, all of this required manual monitoring and break fix using on-site representatives. It was quite common for the computer room to have a control center, known as a NOC (Network Operations Center), with one or more employees manning it twenty-four hours a day.

Today, however, devices within the computer room contain monitoring applications which report back to monitoring services every minute of every day, three hundred and sixty-five days a year. Datacenters are leveraging virtualization for both physical and logical aspects to have best in class Service Level Agreements with their customers on software applications performance and response time while at the same time reducing the needed investments to build redundancy and high availability PODs (Point of delivery).

For example, a typical computer room includes several SAN (Storage Area Network) disk cabinets. Each of these cabinets can hold as many as five hundred disk drives or solid-state disks. With this many components, there is bound to be a failure now and then. They also come equipped with controllers, switches, and other devices which can also fail.

Modern cabinets need to be monitored, from the large variety of sensors, to its environment and general functioning to ensure optimal operations.

In the event of power fluctuations or failures, uneven temperatures, moisture or even too much dust, an alarm will be sent out to third-party operators in the cloud, who will then contact local staff or dispatch someone to fix the problem.

For equipment, algorithms can predict failures before they happen, and send out alarms to the same operators, who can schedule an appointment with the local staff for a technician to come in and solve the issue.

Virtualization has also made it possible to reduce the level of redundancy needed at the physical level while at the same time accelerated the need to have more information across all the value chain to deliver the expected SLAs.

These monitoring and break fix capabilities can justify monthly or yearly recurring charges for maintenance and service contracts. The internal IT staff can rest easy knowing that they will be notified quickly of any issues, most likely before there is a problem, and help can be on the way quickly and efficiently.

Companies with vertical/segment models position themselves as providers of the answer to the need that end users have of high performance, high availability, cross IoT layers stickiness in order to avoid issues before they affect their operations.

The scenario of the data center is an example of what specific segment value can be provided by being connected from an end to end point of view, and customizing this system to deliver specific functions and/or performance to answer specific needs. Take this example and extend it to other industrial applications such as in the oil industry or in a hospital setting; you then have a segment/vertical IoT solution. Ensuring reliability from an end to end perspective factoring it by the value that it brings and costs that the individual is willing to pay for this SLA is easily understandable. For example, in the medical world, a failure can result in the death of a patient, and a factory closure can cause wide-scale job and asset losses.

Not only can IoT prevent failures, the vast quantities of data that can be gathered and stored in the cloud can be analyzed to determine how to improve service, operational trends, and areas of the factory or business.

It's critical that IoT service organizations and manufacturers consider both interoperability and data analytics. This allows the services delivered by single products to be magnified many times over, as well as to justify recurring fee structures.

Performance and service level agreements in this business model are sold as a service with recurring charges to provide customers with service level agreements and the performance they demand. This enables IoT manufacturers to not only generate more income, but to create a steady and predictable stream of revenue which benefits both the IoT companies as well as their customers. The customers receive better service from the analysis of the data as well as the monitoring of the equipment and the manufacturers gain supplemental cash flow streams.

CHAPTER 8

IOT^4 METHODOLOGY
STEP 4:
FROM CUSTOMER EXPERIENCE TO DIGITAL
SAVVY ORGANIZATIONS

"if you really want to create a digital culture in your company, that's everyone's problem."
Kate Smaje, McKinsey Senior Partner

A recent survey among 282 business leaders from three target industries (healthcare, financial services and telecommunications) conducted by the "The Economist Intelligence Unit Limited 2016" (113) shows that the respondents consider that the four greatest changes that their organizations must make to achieve their digital transformation are:

- Increase senior leadership sponsorship and oversight (40%)
- Establish the right organization and governance model (39%)
- Increase funding (37%)
- And finding or developing the necessary talent (34%)

The Internet of Things is very often understood as a way for companies to accelerate:

- Their differentiation by providing unique value propositions to their customers and partners at an acceptable price
- Their financial performance
- Their employees, customers and partners satisfaction

All of this is true, but the final goal should be to deliver an exceptional customer experience. Customers pay the bills; if you can leverage the digitization of the market landscape in which you operate to deliver a better experience at a lower cost, you will be putting odds on your side.

FROM CUSTOMER EXPERIENCE (IOT^4 METHODOLOGY STARTPOINT-STEP 0)

It's not the technology that drives financial performance and customer satisfaction: it's the experience, the enchantment.

Guy Kawasaki, the investor, author, and former Apple "chief evangelist," in his book, *Enchantment: The Art of Changing Hearts, Minds, and Actions* (43), highlights that businesses must go beyond satisfying customers, they must delight them in a unique way that mixes likability, trust and products.

Put your self in the shoes of the customers: this is the start point to any digital transformation. Digital transformation should not have any other purpose than to deliver unique value propositions and experience at the most efficient and maximum price that the customers accept to pay for.

We have previously defined the start point to the IoT^4 strategic methodology as a pre-requisite to the method. The expected outputs of the start point are a clear understanding of:

- your customers' pain points and benefits he expects.
- your current value propositions.
- the gaps between the current customer experience and what it should be.
- brake down the gaps of your customer experience into specific "customer experience moves" that are customer centric.

...TO DIGITIZATION... (IOT⁴ METHODOLOGY STEP 1 TO 3)

The next 3 steps (step 1: making your analog portfolio IoT compatible, step 2: defining an offering differentiation strategy to avoid commoditization and step 3: choosing the most relevant business models) help digitize your existing analog portfolio as well as define differentiation strategies and associated business models.

Step 1 to 3 ensures that:

- all your current analog portfolio components are mapped in the IoT layered structure,
- you define differentiation strategies for each move,
- you have clarity on which business model apply to which move.

...TO CLOSING THE LOOP (IOT⁴ METHODOLOGY STEP 4)

Step 4 is about closing the loop between the results of the 3 steps and your previously defined customer experience moves. It gives you a map of all your individual moves. Each individual move should be equal to a customer value proposition / gain. The sum of all moves should form together the targeted customer experience.

In step 4 you must close the loop with the start point.

Step 4 is about looking back at your "customer experience moves" expressed in a customer centric form/value, and making sure that your IoT moves that take both technologies, business model and differentiation strategies answer your specific customer needs and pain points.

STEP 4:
From customer experience
to digital savvy organizations

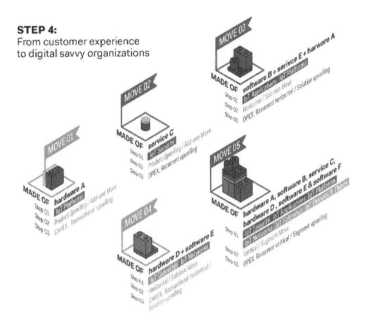

You must make sure that once you have put all your IoT components together (hardware, software and services) for a specific move, that once you have clarified which differentiation strategy and business best apply, that the overall sum answers specific customer needs.

Proof of concepts should be used to identify the potential gaps between what you thought was the customer pain points and how your IoT move answers them. This helps identifying potential gaps or incorrect placements in your portfolio as well as trigger discussions between offer managers and strategy teams to refine the strategic intents and directions.

After the moves and proof of concepts have been validated, comes the execution. Execution needs to be fine-tuned for each organization, each market, competitive landscape and so forth. Our objective is to highlight the importance of having a portfolio strategy but to also consider when defining the execution plan, some important ingredients such as leadership & people and digital savvy organizations.

FROM ANALOG TO DIGITAL SAVVY ORGANIZATIONS

Even though IoT is a technology evolution, keep in mind that examining data from the past will become less and less effective as time goes on.

Thinking that strategizing your digitization moves using the IOT[4] METHODOLOGY is enough is wrong; it's in fact just the beginning.

Olli-Pekka Kallasvuo, former CEO of Nokia, highlighted that "Strategy is 5 percent thinking, 95 percent execution. Strategy execution is 5 percent technical, 95 percent people-related." (Quy Huy, INSEAD Associate Professor of Strategy and Timo Vuori, Assistant Professor of Strategic Management, Aalto University on March 13, 2014 at the INSEAD conference interviewing Olli-Pekka Kallasvuo, former CEO of Nokia).

Senior leadership sponsorship and oversight is needed to digitally transform a customer experience, an existing portfolio and turn an analog savvy organization into a digital savvy organization.

THE IMPORTANCE OF ^{IoT} DIGITAL SAVVY ORGANIZATIONS

Digitization increases employee retention

Planning to leave within one year:

4%
of employees
of digital savy organizations
within 1 year

vs.

20%
of employees of
non digital savy organizations

Digitalization strategies should be embedded into the overall company strategy to leverage its benefits

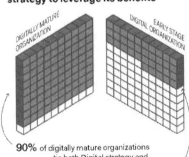

90% of digitally mature organizations
tie both Digital strategy and
overall company strategy
vs. **35%** of early stage digital organization

Digitalization attracts New Talents

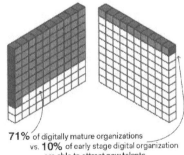

71% of digitally mature organizations
vs. **10%** of early stage digital organization
are able to attract new talents

162

THE IMPORTANCE OF THE HOW

As stated in previous chapters, analog leaders that must deal with digital transformation of their business model (including the consequences and potential disruptions of IoT) are faced with four possible choices:

- Ignore
- Milk the cow
- U-turn the mothership
- Transforming from the edge

Considering that:

- Digitization and IoT can drive your financial performance
- That "transforming from the edge" is the right strategy for your company to leap frog your competition
- to avoid commoditization, you need to adapt your current analog offer portfolio to make it more "IoT compatible". You must also define offering differentiation strategies and choose the most relevant business models.

You still need to clarify the how. In other words, how will you make it happen and are there different options? Typically, once you have clarified your strategic moves, the next question you should ask is 'How will I execute the transformation'?

There are five execution strategies (none is mutually exclusive) when dealing with digital transformation which perfectly apply to the "transforming from the edge" strategic option (8):

Build

Building is a good option if you are ready to create internal start-ups from the core of your organization. Studies show that teams operating independently from their parents are more innovative and have higher market-penetration rates than those that were kept integrated (105). Companies wanting to transform from the core or even from the edge but with non-autonomous ventures or organizations, underperform those with separated entities. Even fully autonomous ventures need to be treated as start-up's by:

- Limited step funding and strong financial oversight to avoid the "no money and time limit" syndrome that internal start-ups in big corporations very often face.
- Appoint senior managers, risk, compliance and control 'relationship managers' with an entrepreneurial and pro-active attitude to work closely together with the start-up.
- Let the start-up make its own decisions in running their business in all its aspects—technology, operations, HR, etc. aspects.

Acquire – Buy

If you need to move quickly you may find yourself following an acquisition strategy to purchase your way into the new paradigm. Acquiring is not a strategy; it's about the synergy with the acquired company, in a way to ideally accomplish your strategic move.

Partner or Ally

Another option is to partner with other businesses to build alliances which move your corporation into the new paradigm. Partnering or Alliances to enhance joint development relationships can be a very productive way to accelerate your market penetration if the counterpart has made the same effort to clarify his strategic options and moves to tackle what IoT's accessible growth can create.

Invest

Invest in companies which will help move your business towards the digital revolution. Putting in place the venture capital for early and later venture investments should facilitate market access or joint development agreements.

Co-develop

Work with developers all over the world to help you create the IoT products and services you will need.

THE IMPORTANCE OF INTERNAL COMMUNICATION AND STORY TELLING

As stated before, we do not want to give any guidance regarding which execution strategy might be best suited in each case and company. However, this resource's detailed description will give you a relevant list of options.

When you have defined which IoT strategy fits your circumstances and the associated execution strategy, your next hurdle is the internal communication you need to put in place to streamline your execution.

Explaining the 'Why' and the 'How' are as important as defining them.

Usually companies focus on their customers, on their channels and on their branding towards those who sell and buy their products, software, services and so forth. However, they often underestimate the importance of internal communication. It is vital for companies to explain to their employees the how and the why.

Unfortunately, the attitude often is "Employees are there to be doing what they are told, so why bother explaining to them the how and the why?" If this is your belief – if this is how you perceive the core resource of an enterprise – then change management will not be your cup of tea. Change is all about people and it is all about communicating and enhancing change in the mind of people the enterprise stands for. If you wish to drive and succeed in change management, then communication is at the core.

Chip Heath and Dan Heath, in their book *Made to Stick* (114), shed the light about the importance of internal communication towards employees when there are strategic choices made that require changes in behaviors as well as the understandings that trigger those. They highlight in particular the importance of guiding those behaviors: "If your frontline employees can talk about your strategy, can tell stories about it, can talk back to their managers and feel credible doing so, then the strategy is doing precisely what it was intended to do: guide behavior (114)".

Tell your strategy as a story to make it realistic and understandable for middle management. Use a common language to be understood by all your company's employees. Being practical and down to earth are important aspects of useful communication when dealing with change. If you are a leader of a legacy analog company, you must perfect these communications.

IT STARTS WITH PEOPLE

Even though the digital transformation has been building up for over a decade, most businesses have yet to recognize it as a high priority. This is especially true of larger corporations with solid, apparently unassailable channels and markets.

It is true that some businesses will not be impacted by what IoT brings to the table. But are you truly confident, as you read these sentences, that your business is immune to the IoT revolution?

Many leaders may not see the threats to their business and are blinded by their current analog profitability. Our brain is "inherently lazy" and will always "choose the most energy efficient path" if we let it, writes Tara Swart, a senior lecturer at MIT, in her book *Neuroscience for Leadership* (115). "[The brain's] need [to survive] focuses attention on the sources of danger and on trying to predict where the next threat will appear, on escape or full-frontal battle rather than on an innovative or creative solution, on avoiding risk rather than managing it towards a new suite of products, market or way of doing business" Swart writes.

If leaders don't see the threat and opportunities of the IoT and fail to understand how they can leverage it for their company's benefit, then they are in danger of becoming yet another case study like Kodak, Nokia, and Polaroid.

On the other side of the coin, there are leaders who fully acknowledge that there are some risks and that those might be potentially deadly to their business. They struggle to raise the urgency of change and the associated orchestration among their employees. When properly tackled, digital transformation can ignite a sense of purpose among your teams, and more importantly raise the overall satisfaction and therefore increase their buy-in from them which often increases productivity. Studies show that when a clear digital strategy is being established and shared with employees, the satisfaction of those employees raises from 10% to nearly 90% (108).

The importance of leadership

John Kotter, Professor of Leadership, Emeritus, at the Harvard Business School, author of numerous books on leadership, highlights this importance of leadership and the difference between leadership and management when dealing with change management (116):

- Management gets the regular work done well, reliably and efficiently, even in exceptionally large and complex systems.
- Leadership sets the vision and the associate strategy. They have the capability to energize their troops to trigger innovation despite the recognized changing problems and opportunities.

Both are important when dealing with a digital transformation strategy in a complex environment and organization. Leadership is a key success factor when dealing with market niche or in a world where opportunities and technological trends can change greatly. Good management is a key success factor in large organizations operating in protected markets and environments that change little (117).

THE IMPORTANCE OF LEADERSHIP & PEOPLE

KEY ATTRIBUTES OF DIGITAL LEADERS

22% TRANSFORMATIVE VISION

22% COLLABORATIVE SKILLS

20% FORWARD THINKING

18% CHANGE-ORIENTED MINDSET

The importance of digital mine canaries

Another important aspect when dealing with people in a digital transformation environment is that there is often someone who will understand the necessary steps to digital transformation before the rest of the peers and thus challenge the status quo. Those within the corporation who recognize the need for change often face marginalization from the minds of the "analog" leaders and skepticism from peers.

Carl Yankoswki joined Polaroid in 1988 as Vice President in charge of the business imaging, U.S. consumers and industrial marketing.

He quickly identified the necessity for Polaroid to embrace the digital transformation by acquiring electronic imaging technologies. Unfortunately, MacAllister Booth (118), his CEO, vetoed the plan and gave clear "analog" feedback, "Anyone who says instant photography is dying has his head in the sand". Even the next CEO, Gary DiCamillo, had a very similar analog approach. He stated in 2008 at a Yale interview that "People were betting on hard copy and media that was going to be pick-up-able, visible, see able, touchable, as a photograph would be". A couple of years later he analyzed the situation: "We knew we needed to change the fan belt, but we couldn't stop the engine. And the reason we couldn't stop the engine was that instant film was the core of the financial model of this company". This is very similar to Fujifilm's model; the major difference is that Fujifilm's management made a clear strategic choice to cannibalize their own market in order to enable the transformation to happen and build a longer term success.

Such an environment unleashes the opportunity to get early warning detection systems for your business, much like a canary in a coal mine. So, keep in mind that the canaries are not the problem. Rather, it's the way you, as a leader and as a company, leverage them to create value for your customers, your channels, your company and its employees and the shareholders (119).

Carl Yankoswki was Polaroid's canary, and unfortunately for them, he was ignored.

Polaroid could have been a pioneer in digital photography if the leaders had embraced original ideas and set a vision that included the understanding that failing fast, protecting teams that challenge the status quo, embracing culture change can create the conditions for successful digital transformation. Unfortunately, Polaroid failed in those areas mainly because they did not have the conditions for its employees to embrace change and accelerate the needed digital transformation. This example highlights the importance of the people side of digital transformation and in particular the role of middle management when dealing with change and adaptation of organizations.

The importance of middle management

When dealing with digital transformation, leadership must first set a vision and clearly state and envision the result of the changes that are necessary. But vision and leadership are not enough. The Polaroid case clearly shows that even though they had performed thorough market research, even though they could have acquired the technology and even though they had leaders that had perceived the opportunity behind the risk, they did not realize the importance of middle management in digital transformation.

George Casper Homans was an American Sociologist (August 11, 1910 – May 29, 1989), founder of behavioral sociology and the Social Exchange Theory. He expressed in his different publications the importance of middle status of individuals in social organizations as well as their capabilities to absorb and drive creativity (120) (121).

He considers that any hierarchical social organization is constituted of:

- "Low status individuals": individuals that do not fear status loss as they feel that they do not have anything to lose. Status can be defined as respect, honor, influence on other groups with the associate benefits such as credit, control, attention, influence as well as material benefits.

170

- "High status individuals": interestingly high-status individuals have a very similar reaction to their social status in that they are not afraid of losing social esteem, but not because of the same reasons. The consequence of being at the top of the social pyramid are the associate advantages such as ego satisfaction, financial freedom and well-being which in turn gives those individuals a lot of freedom in their everyday life and decisions.
- "Middle status individuals": Those individuals are on the opposite side, when talking about fear of losing status, of both the low and high-status individuals. The threat of status loss is the highest in this category of individuals as they are respected and can influence the low status individuals while at the same time dealing with the high-status individuals that are more respected and influential to the whole group.

If you apply those categories to a standard medium size company, you could categorize the groups as follows:

- "Low-status individuals": skilled or semiskilled workers, administrative personnel, transversal function with low influential power, etc.
- "High-status individuals": executive teams and their associate N-1. Transversal functions with influential power.
- "Middle-status individuals": middle management that refer to high status individuals to seek for approval and or final decisions, etc.

Middle management and innovation

Recent studies seem to show that when dealing with innovation, transformation and change in a social organization such as a company, the middle status individuals will be more concerned than other groups to follow the rules at the cost of creativity and innovation. From an innovation point of view (organizational, R&D, process and so forth), being criticized and negatively evaluated for suggesting creative ideas may be particularly salient to middle status individuals. Middle status individuals tend to be less creative than those with high or low status but on the other side they can boost the group's performance by focusing on productive tasks and filtering out irrelevant information (120).

High status individuals seem to have more willingness to risk the expression of creative ideas due to the fact that they are well established as high status individuals and do not fear of losing their position. Interestingly Michelle M. Duguid and Jack Goncalo in their article "Squeezed in the Middle: The Middle Status Trade Creativity for Focus" study seem also to show that, even if the high-status individuals' creative ideas are objectively not more creative than ideas from the middle or low status individuals, their status and associate confidence makes them more confident to persuade the rest of the group.

In the Polaroid case, middle management didn't embrace the high-status individuals' beliefs and because of that they were pushed to the side. This caused major issues with innovation, digital transformation, cohesion and keeping digital talents in the company.

Analog company Leaders willing to embrace the IoT should help the company's middle management to understand the goals and outcomes, as well as the risks and threats to the existing business.

Setting a vision and giving a sense to the mission is not only about defining what needs to be done but also about creating the environment in which employees can challenge and enhance the status quo on very diverse subjects such as the business model, processes, products and services.

Explaining the "why" to middle management and more importantly enabling innovative action in the edge of the "mothership" creates the environment for change and adds a sense of urgency and accountability amongst the middle status individuals.

Even if middle status individuals seem to be more concerned than other groups about following the rules at the cost of creativity and innovation, other studies suggest that middle managers can be very valuable contributors to the execution and the realization of a digital transformation within the company. Unfortunately, middle management contributions in digital transformation are often unrecognized or not valued enough by most senior executives. Quy Nguyen Huy in his article *In Praise of Middle Managers* from the September 2001 issue of *Harvard Business Review* (122), highlights the fact that those contributions occur in four areas:

- First, middle managers if given the proper hearing from the high management can not only propose entrepreneurial ideas but are also willing to execute.
- Second, middle managers very often can leverage their informal networks at a wider scale than high management and can leverage it to implement substantive and lasting change.
- Third, middle managers can maintain the transformation momentum amongst employees to whom they are connected on a daily basis
- Finally, middle managers manage to keep the organization executing its primary role while at the same time transforming it from the inside.

Let's have a look at another well-known company that underestimated the importance of middle management and because of that, nearly vanished: Nokia. This resilient giant has managed to go through major transformations throughout its history since 1865: from rubber and paper to cable, from cable to mobile phones, from mobile phone to mobile internet. Nokia was one of the leading manufacturers in mobile technologies producing over 100,000,000 mobile phones in 1998. So, what happened?

On March 13, 2014 at the INSEAD conference Quy Nguyen Huy, INSEAD Associate Professor of Strategy and Timo Vuori, Assistant Professor of Strategic Management at Aalto University interviewed Olli-Pekka

Kallasvuo, former CEO of Nokia on this subject (123). Their resume on Mr Kallasvuo feedbacks were clear: "The problem of Nokia, after all, seems frustratingly similar to those of many large companies such as Microsoft or Sony who could not develop high quality innovative products fast enough to match their rising competitors. As the companies grew larger and richer, each department became its own kingdom, each executive a little emperor and people were more concerned about their status and internal promotion than cooperating actively with other departments to produce innovative products rapidly. (...) the overriding emotion felt by top managers and middle managers within the organization was one of fear. And yet, it wasn't necessarily a fear of being fired which pervaded; it was more about fear of losing social status in the organization (123)".

MANAGING CHANGE

Protecting the Mothership

Obviously, it is vital that the "mothership", the analog corporation, is protected during the transformation in order to let the transformation teams understand the new market and rules of the game. Nonetheless, the analog corporations that identify potential threats must adapt to the new rules of the games, if applicable, and even be willing to pivot hard, in order to prosper in their new environment.

To address the change management needed to transform from the edge, we highlight the need to rely on respected research on that specific subject. One of the most respected authorities on change management, John Kotter professor at the Harvard Business School, observed countless leaders and organizations as they were trying to transform or execute their strategies. He identified and extracted the success factors and combined them into a methodology with 8 simple steps (124) with the first step being to establish a sense of urgency. Other steps include the clarification and communication of the vision and the associate strategy as well as empowering employees to implement short term wins to anchor the change management. John Kotter emphasizes the role of leadership when addressing change management and how important it is for them to be attentive to disengagement and a complacent behavior that can make you think that what got you here will get you there.

The importance of the sense of urgency

Clark Gilbert and Joseph L. Bower in their *Disruptive Change: When Trying Harder Is Part of the Problem* highlighted that in order to leverage disruptive innovations, companies may need to rework and/or redesign existing organizations, cost structures, business models, channels, product portfolio and so forth. If only threat-induced rigidity is used towards the organization to enhance change, the company as a whole will have a tendency to push harder on previously successful paths instead of trying to find a new direction (105)".

Thus, not only does the middle management need to see the IoT as a threat and an opportunity but also as an innovation, or to be more precise, an evolution of the M2M digital transformation that requires their attention. Having middle management understand the importance of the IoT for the company and the associated sense of urgency to address it all is an important step in digital transformation.

The IoT needs to be discussed by middle management as both:

- A threat: to ensure proper resources and funding are allocated
- An opportunity: to motivate middle management to find unique applications associated with the innovation

If the sense of urgency is not well understood, the risk rises because middle management does not see the IoT as critical or a priority.

The most effective way to get middle management to listen is to have the proof brought to them by their peers. Therefore, if both the threat and the sense of urgency are not understood, then create small middle management teams whose purpose will be to raise both the sense of urgency and the possible threat by "hacking" your core business.

THE IMPORTANCE OF R&D

As stated in chapter 5, technologies related to the IoT and IoT standards will dramatically evolve soon.

Defining a move from an analog to an IoT compatible portfolio is only half the path to digitizing your portfolio. The key element is your execution arm: the research and development teams. To transform an analog portfolio, R&D organizations will be facing important challenges concerning the competency of their resources and regarding the overall bandwidth available to transform an already existing portfolio. These teams will also be facing strategic choices about interoperability, transitioning existing customers into the IoT space, and innovation.

IoT brings constraints to R&D teams regarding speed, agility and short design cycles as well as retaining current analog employees and attracting new digital talents needed to accelerate change. There is currently a high need for digital, IoT-savvy talent, very like what happened with the Internet between the years 1995 and 2000.

Even though IoT is a technology evolution, keep in mind that examining data from the past will become less and less effective as time goes on. IoT is different than M2M because of its scale and speed.

Whatever IoT strategy you choose, scale and speed will impact your organization, including sales and marketing. The most impacted will be the R&D teams.

To keep up with IoT Technologies, R&D teams will have to reduce the time between the identification of a specific need and the launch of the product or service that fulfills it. Agile and Scrum are well adapted to markets that require R&D teams to quickly respond to changing customer needs and innovation.

Scrum is a general management methodology coinciding with the Agile movement in software development, which is partly inspired by Lean manufacturing approaches such as the Toyota Production System.

AGILE DEVELOPMENT

Waterfall Model

Agile Model

progress

| Physical Design |
| Software |
| Verification |
| Design |
| Specification |

progress

| Physical Design |
| Software |
| Verification |
| Design |
| Specification |

The main challenges when accelerating speed and scale in established analog R&D organizations is the need to leverage best-in-class methods and processes that drive innovation and enable more people to work together.

Scrum is appropriate for work with uncertain requirements and/or uncertain technology issues, which is what the IoT brings to the table:

Baba Shiv, Professor of Marketing at Stanford Graduate School of Business whose research focuses on innovation in the workplace, highlighted that "If you're trying to solve a problem there are potentially hundreds of possible pathways to take, but only a few are going to lead to the appropriate solution. And the only way to discover that is to try and fail and try again (125)".

Innovation requires plenty of trial and error, and the Agile model enables failure to occur more quickly and on a smaller scale. Enabling teams to fail and accelerating the time to failure drives innovation in product development and design, in associated business models, ecosystems, and so forth.

But the well-known mantra, "failing fast", has restrictions and is a narrow-minded approach of innovation. R&D teams face this issue in their everyday work.

The reality is that if you are an established "Analog" organization, you don't get to make an unlimited number of bets on the marketplace because at some point there needs to be some commitment on resources at an enterprise scale. Unfortunately established analog organizations have limited resources to drive the digital transformation of their core analog offerings portfolio. They cannot create thousands of internal start-ups or give an unlimited budget to R&D; an established enterprise doesn't have this luxury.

These companies must often bear the cost of legacy analog systems, break through regulatory barriers, marshal multi-disciplinary teams and try to drive innovation at the same time.

That's why transforming from the edge and innovation must work together. IoT will have different impacts on R&D teams, often challenging the core products of what is being researched and developed, sometimes only at the edge.

Established analog R&D departments may have the capabilities and the expertise to innovate to the level of speed required by IoT. That is why, for whatever option you choose, you will need to give clarity to your different R&D teams about what innovation means and in which arena you want each of them to play. Use the IoT architecture layer to initiate discussions and decisions on which direction you want to evolve and invest in.

THE IMPORTANCE OF INTERNAL HACKATHONS AND INTERNAL HACKERS

Company operations are getting more automated using tools such as PRM, CRM, ERPs, and so on. The IoT will bring even more automation due to the number of connected things, gateways, cloud based software and intelligence. Analog R&D departments often consider that being compliant with the latest security standards is enough. In the analog world products, protocols and architectures are often proprietary, making hacking difficult. The challenge that the IoT brings is that it will expose your offer; this will force your R&D teams to develop products that are more open and standardized. Consequently, it will expose your portfolio to more security issues.

Jeff Jarmoc tweeted: "In a relatively short time we've taken a system built to resist destruction by nuclear weapons and made it vulnerable to toasters (126)".

The main challenge is understanding and anticipating security threats and building products. Creating services, hardware and software that are developed in a way that they can be upgraded to address the changing security landscape. Security must be embedded throughout the process and not just slapped on at the end as an option or afterthought, at the end of the R&D activity.

Hackathons were established to address this gap and should be part of the overall R&D effort for the following reasons.

- You release better products because your own engineering teams find the holes and vulnerabilities of your core offer instead of competition or malicious hackers.
- You create an environment where engineering teams can generate ideas without the burden of other engineers, product managers, tools and processes which enhances change and innovation.
- You create the condition for cross team sharing, building and collaboration.

- This enables your company to brand itself as open and friendly to developers. The importance of developing communities is a factor in the success of IoT products and is clearly an accelerator to market differentiation.
- This attracts millennials and digital talents to accelerate the digital transformation of your organization.

Hacking teams need to be built with millennials and digital natives. This in turn will accelerate the digital transformation of your organization and make it more responsive to changes in the IoT marketplace.

To keep up the momentum, schedule a hackathon every quarter. For example, Facebook schedules hackathons every 8 to 10 weeks.

THE IMPORTANCE OF DIGITAL DIVERSITY ACROSS GENERATIONS

As a business is transformed from the edge, one of the challenges is managing the various teams throughout the organization. This includes existing staff within the analog business plus those team members dedicated to the new digital technology plus staff that straddles both worlds.

Younger people, who tend to be digital natives, often have a much greater affinity for new technologies and rapid change, while members of the older generations often have a deep understanding of the business, its processes, channels and markets. On the other hand, those same young people may be viewed as unproductive and unreliable.

Do not underestimate the clash of cultures between generations but also realize the great opportunity that resides when mixing different generations with a common purpose towards digital transformation.

It is vital to encourage cooperation between the disparate generational understandings of team members. You can improve overall productivity by putting in place programs to help people to work more closely together and have a greater understanding for each other's strengths and weaknesses through these different approaches.

THE IMPORTANCE OF IoT DIGITAL SAVVY ORGANIZATIONS

More Data requires More Developers

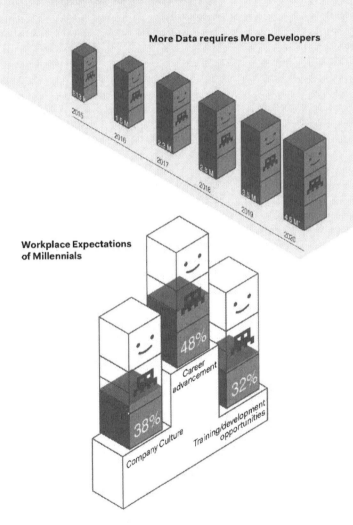

Workplace Expectations of Millennials

THE IMPORTANCE OF DIGITAL TALENT MANAGEMENT

Companies that are faced with digital transformation must address how they attract qualified talent, and keep them motivated and engaged. IoT talents are needed to leap frog your competitors and companies will be fighting each other to attract them.

The key success factor for successful digital transformation is people.

Unfortunately for legacy analog players that have analog human resources, the change is even more drastic than the one Nokia had experienced. IoT will impact your organization by creating new positions and new job descriptions such as Chief Internet of Things Officer (CIoTO); IoT Architects, IoT software engineer, Business Designer; IoT Stack and platform Developer.

To address this need, new training organizations have emerged, such as the IoT Talent Consortium (https://www.IoTtalent.org/) led by Cisco and General Electric, and university certified courses

Millennials are looking for engaging dynamics and interesting career opportunities. According to a World Economic Forum Survey, career advancement (48%), company culture (38%) and training/development opportunities (32%) are important employment considerations for millennials. To retain them, you need to fulfill these objectives so they come on board and remain engaged. (126)

Here is the IoT job trend from www.indeed.com, posted on February 2017 (127):

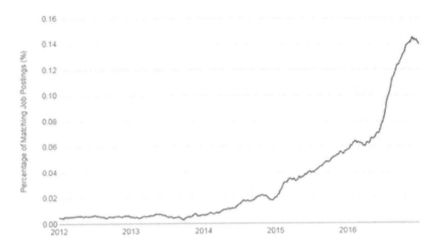

Even though there is clearly a job trend with IoT, one of the challenges faced by businesses today is that graduates from universities and colleges are not educated and trained in the areas required in the modern world. These include subjects such as cybercrime, IoT, robotics, big data, and analytics.

As an analog leader, understanding the IoT's implication on your team and talent diversity is essential. With the IoT market trend, appropriate trained resources will become scarcer and scarcer. Companies need more IoT trained resources and the needs are so big that there never be enough to go around.

During the IoT World Forum 2014, the Internet of Things World Forum leaders announced the creation of the IoT Talent Consortium. The objective of this non-profit organization, is to improve education for the necessary talents, such as hybrid sets of skills, needed to move the industry to a wide-scale development (128). The talent consortium highlights that "there is a projected skills gap of 2 million trained engineers that will be need specialized training over the coming decade to help realize the value of IoT (129)".

Leveraging partnerships with universities to train your future workforce, identifying and attracting the IoT talents from other markets, and retaining those key resources should be on the top of the leader's mind and their human resources leaders.

Digital transformation is about people, attracting the right talents to drive and executing this transformation.

THE IMPORTANCE OF CHANNELS AND IoT PARTNER PROGRAMS

An IoT product strategy needs to take into consideration the very dynamic evolution of the ecosystem and associated channels.

A lot of current analog channels, and mainly the system integrators, will be facing the same paradigm: how to transform their capabilities, competencies while at the same time protecting their services contracts and associated installed based.

Depending on which strategy your analog company wants to implement (horizontal and/or vertical), you might face some important historical channel disruptions while at the same time confronting some newcomers from other markets in your go to markets.

Numerous channels have been relying on legacy or semi-legacy systems to build an entrance barrier for newcomers. Maintenance contracts have been the golden goose for a lot of system integrators. The IoT will very probably force them to move from being hardware installers into more software and service driven companies. Those system integrators will need to leverage their IoT layered architecture's products (such as IoT platforms, advanced services such as analytics, openness to integrate third party hardware and software, etc.) to differentiate. There will still be a huge space for hardware resellers, but the added value of such positioning linked to the commoditization of what was once a very profitable market will be a blessing for wholesalers and low margin/high volume companies.

Analog manufacturers that take this evolution into account with regard to their partner's business models and support them into this transition through their channel program and operations will not only secure their current market share but also extend the accessible market share.

Designing efficient IoT partner programs to help your historical partners cross the chasm from analog expertise to digital expertise as well as attracting new partners into your channels should be part of any digitization strategy.

Digitization of the channel is often put as the last item on the list; it should be fully part of the product design phase to successfully launch your IoT offers. "IoT ready" Channels should be a core element of your IoT strategy. An offer with a poor competent channel is the recipe for disaster. Products and demand generation activities are useless if there are no channels to fulfill and relay the demand.

THE IMPORTANCE OF ECOSYSTEMS AND ALLIANCES

The Importance of ecosystems

Analog manufacturers have very often developed their products as all-in-one systems with waterproof openness (i.e.: with very strict and controlled interoperability.)

An important aspect, when executing an IoT strategy, is to consider ecosystems such as those used by developers because modern competitive battles are won by attracting developers. You just must look at all the major players such as Google, Apple, Amazon, Facebook, and Salesforce: they differentiate by enabling others to develop in their controlled yet flexible ecosystem.

We think that, due to the speed of how the IoT will move, future IoT winners will be decided by the developers. Understanding their needs and taking those into account when defining your IoT strategy will enable your company to accelerate the time when others will be stuck with a non-ecosystem friendly offer. If you succeed in making your current analog offerings embrace the IoT through the developer's lenses and create the environment for them to expand the capabilities of your offerings, you will, without a doubt, leap frog your competition and beat commoditization of your products.

The difficulty for current analog leaders will be to move their core offerings that have not been, at the origin, created and designed to facilitate the creation and sustainability of a wide ecosystem of developers.

A classic scenario is an analog manufacturer willing to leverage the IoT to differentiate and grow. The most logical move for them would be to embed, in its portfolio, more and more IT capabilities; but unfortunately, this is not enough. An analog company willing to move into the IT space needs to consider not only the technology but also the associated channels and ecosystem. Maximizing technology stickiness between products from different companies is an efficient strategy to gain market share and develop a compelling IoT story.

187

Cisco technologies and protocols comply with different standards as well as a list of key differentiated technologies and protocols that is unique to their offer. The objective of the following examples is to highlight that an OT analog company willing to go into the IT space, will need its employees to master not only the acronyms and the technologies but also the ecosystems that both worlds possess. Cisco, for example, has developed differentiated technologies and protocol to complement standards in order to beat commoditization and bring more added value to its resellers and end users. These include offers such as Identity Services Engine (130) to simplify guest experiences (131), as well as Smart Install that provides zero-touch deployment for new switches.

The IoT will both require and enable more stickiness between the OT (Operational Technologies) and IT (Information Technologies) worlds. Unfortunately, this will come at a cost for Research and Development teams from both sides, OT and IT, to understand that their offers will need to be compliant with both the channels' requirements and expectations as well as the ecosystems that exist in the go to market. This is driven by the necessity of the channel partner to leverage an ecosystem of products and services in order to maximize added value and differentiate themselves.

When you look at the three strategic moves (addressed in Chapter 6), Product Upselling / Add-ons Move; Horizontal / Solution Move, and the Vertical / Segment Move, you understand that to be able to successfully leverage those moves, your organization will need to work within an ecosystem. This ecosystem will be comprised of other manufacturers, software providers, partners and channels.

Understanding the requirements of this ecosystem will be a key success factor. Building unique value propositions with them is an important step to beat commoditization of your portfolio and drive the demand generation for end users towards it.

The importance of alliances

Channels and ecosystems are important parts of collaboration with your go to market and all associated aspects of it such as the development communities that enhance your portfolio. Alliances also must be taken into consideration when executing your IoT strategy.

Alliances are crucial for companies competing in the IoT space. This is due to the speed at which innovations are taking place and the fact that the IoT market will structure itself as the IT market has been organizing itself in the last 30 years. This is true not only from a technical standpoint but also from a go to market and co-competition type of relationships between the different actors.

We highly recommend that, as part of your execution strategy, you consider and assess the opportunity to negotiate win-win agreements. Alliances are not about dividing the pie that is not growing but instead building incremental value and extending the size of the pie to grow as a result (130).

CHAPTER 9

USING THE IOT⁴ METHODOLOGY

"Have no fear of perfection. You'll never reach it."
Salvador Dali

START POINT (STEP 0): YOUR CUSTOMERS

Although technology isn't the only catalyst for digital transformation, companies see the IoT as a form of progress to deliver better customer experiences.

One of the best ways to succeed in the "transformation from the edge" of your business in this digital age is to focus on your customers by understanding and controlling every point where the customers are involved in any way. By understanding these intersections, you can model your processes to provide the optimum experience for your customers. Additionally, this will give you information and inputs about customer behavior which you can use to judge whether your changes are working and if they need to be modified.

Customers interface with your business at many different points. Obviously, they make a purchase, but there is much more to the process than paying for products or services.

In today's world, consumers are heavily involved in social media, and use various social channels such as Facebook, Google, Amazon, LinkedIn and YouTube to decide what to purchase and to report on the quality of products and services that they received. It is vital that you consider all the digital marketing aspects of your products and services because your customers will use them regardless of whether or not you do.

The customer journey, through physical and digital touchpoints, should be your starting point. More importantly understand your customer's path to purchase.

To make matters more complicated, sometimes the customer is not the consumer. This is very well illustrated by toys, where the customer is the parent and the consumer is the child. Lars Silberbauer, Global Director of Social Media and Search at Lego™ (131). said, "Shoppers are not the same as consumers. Consumers are usually kids without the ability to buy things. At the same time, we want them to tell their parents, and we want their parents to have a good experience as they shop. As a result, there are two different consumer journeys here."

Showing and demonstrating a customer-centric culture and approach is the compass that guides the organization towards a successful digital transformation, leveraging both the risks and the opportunities to leapfrog the competition.

You should not start the first step without having a clear understanding of your "customer experience moves" expressed in a customer centric form/value. Alan Smith, Alexander Osterwalder, Greg Bernarda, Gregory Bernarda, Trish Papadakos, and Yves Pigneur in their book Value Proposition Design: How to Create Products and Services Customers Want (44) consider that a good way to express a direction of your value proposition is to express it using this template: Our (products and services) help(s) (customer segment) who want to (jobs to be done) by (your own verb) and (your own verb). Unlike (competing value proposition).

The sum of all moves should form together the targeted customer experience.

STEP 1: MAKING YOUR ANALOG PORTFOLIO IOT COMPATIBLE

The first step consists of assessing which portion of your current core offer (hardware, software, and services) you think would be good candidates for the IoT. Once you have listed all potential suspects, you need to unbundle them to map them and assess where to place them, in at least one of the six IoT technological layers:

Vertical:
1. IoT Devices & Things.
2. IoT Gateways.
3. IoT Platforms.
4. IoT Users Access and Applications.

Transversals:
5. IoT Networks (wired and wireless).
6. IoT Security.

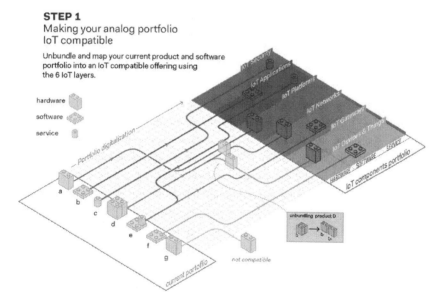

STEP 1
Making your analog portfolio
IoT compatible

Unbundle and map your current product and software
portfolio into an IoT compatible offering using
the 6 IoT layers.

The objective when unbundling your existing products / offer is to identify which portion of your offer fits which layer of the IoT framework. Getting your current offer IoT compatible means that you need to unbundle your current offer to the most unique product that maximizes return for both vendor and customer. This means that by doing this you end up with the minimal offer bricks that fulfil customer needs and solve their problem at a cost they are willing to pay. This means that there is nothing in the brick that answers more than just what is expected and paid for. By breaking down your offer in such a way, you create the conditions to define and implement a differentiation strategy to avoid commoditization.

The results in assessing, unbundling and mapping your current product and software portfolio into an IoT compatible offering could be represented as the following:

IoT Layers	IoT Portfolio			Not Iot compatible
	Hardware	Software	Service	
IoT Security			Service C	
IoT Applications		Software B	Service E	
IoT Platforms	Hardware A			Hardware G
IoT Network	Hardware D'	Software E		
IoT Gateways	Hardware D''			
IoT Devices		Software F		

IoT⁴ Strategic Methodology – Canvas #1 – offering compatibility mapping (output of step 1)

A product in your current portfolio might need to be broken down into one or more pieces such as hardware, software and services. This also means that there might be some current offerings that might not fit in the IoT layers.

This would mean that you would typically have an IoT compatible matrix for your current portfolio. Once you have clarified which portion of your core offer you want to assess and put in the IoT^4 Strategic Methodology - Canvas #1 - Offering Compatibility Mapping, you need to find a way to understand the different options available to extend the core to avoid falling into the commoditization space. The challenge is finding a simple way to explain to your marketing, sales, R&D teams, and so forth what is feasible and where the current and future offering fits in the IoT architecture/layer landscape.

Our proposal also considers that each company, each core offer, even portion of the core offer might fit well with one or more of those strategic options.

STEP 2: DEFINING OFFERING STRATEGIES

The second step consists of choosing one or an aggregation of your IoT compatible components and defining which differentiation strategy best applies to avoid commoditization of your portfolio. There are mainly 3 types of differentiation strategic moves:

- Product upselling / Add-ons Move
- Horizontal / Solution Move
- Vertical / Segment Move

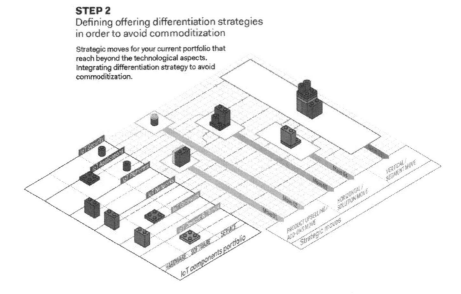

STEP 2
Defining offering differentiation strategies
in order to avoid commoditization

Strategic moves for your current portfolio that
reach beyond the technological aspects.
Integrating differentiation strategy to avoid
commoditization.

You end up with as many moves as needed:

IoT Layers	OFFERING DIFFERENTIATION STRATEGIES - Strategic Moves		
	Product upselling / add-ons Move	Horizontal / Solution Move	Vertical / Segment Move
IoT Security	Move 2		
IoT Applications		Move 3	
IoT Platforms	Move1		Move 5
IoT Network			
IoT Gateways		Move 4	
IoT Devices			

IoT⁴ Strategic Methodology – canvas #2.1 – differentiation strategies to avoid commoditization (output of step 2).

And in a synthetic way:

	OFFERING DIFFERENTIATION STRATEGIES - Strategic Moves type	Number of components	List of components
Move 1	Product upselling / add-ons Move	1	Hardware A
Move 2		1	Product C
Move 3	Horizontal / Solution Move	3	Software B + Service E + Hardware A
Move 4		2	Software E + Hardware D''
Move 5	Vertical / Segment Move	6	Service C + Software B + Hardware A + Software E + Hardware D''+ Software F

IoT⁴ Strategic Methodology – canvas #2.2 – differentiation strategies to avoid commoditization (output of step 2).

You now have clear strategic moves for your current portfolio that embraces not only the way the IoT is structuring itself from a technology perspective, but also a differentiation strategy to avoid commoditization.

STEP 3: CHOOSING THE MOST RELEVANT BUSINESS MODELS

Having followed step 1 and 2, you now should have answers on the following areas:

- Your current portfolio concerned by the IoT.
- Where each component fits in the 6 layers of architecture.
- The different ways you want to bundle those components across those 6 layers. This is called a strategic move.
- The type of differentiation strategies you want to apply to each of those moves.

You now need to clarify which business model fits best your edging strategy.

As defined previously there are 6 possible financial models:

- CAPEX:
  - Transactional upselling
  - Transactional Horizontal / Solution upselling
  - Transactional Vertical / Segment upselling
- OPEX:
  - Recurrent upselling
  - Recurrent Horizontal / Solution upselling
  - Recurrent Vertical / Segment upselling

We now need to clarify which financial model fits best for each strategic move:

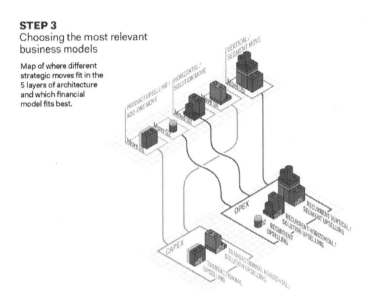

STEP 3
Choosing the most relevant
business models

Map of where different
strategic moves fit in the
5 layers of architecture
and which financial
model fits best.

	OFFERING DIFFERENTIATION STRATEGIES - Strategic Moves type	Type of financial model		
		OPEX	CAPEX	Business Model to apply
Move 1	Product upselling / add-ons Move		Y	Transactional upselling
Move 2		Y		Recurrent upselling
Move 3	Horizontal / Solution Move	Y		Recurrent Horizontal / Solution upselling
Move 4			Y	Transactional Horizontal / Solution upselling
Move 5	Vertical / Segment Move	Y		Recurrent Vertical / Segment upselling

IoT⁴ Strategic Methodology – canvas #3.1 – Business Models per
strategic move (output of step 3).

When merging all the previous information, you end up with a clear map of your different strategic moves. You will also understand where it fits in the 6 layers' architecture and which financial model fits best:

	OFFERING DIFFERENTIATION STRATEGIES - Strategic Moves type	Number of components	List of components	Type of financial model		
				OPEX	CAPEX	Business Model to apply
Move 1	Product upselling / add-ons	1	Hardware A		Y	Transactional upselling
Move 2	Move	1	Product C	Y		Recurrent upselling
Move 3	Horizontal / Solution Move	3	Software B + Service E + Hardware A	Y		Recurrent Horizontal / Solution upselling
Move 4		2	Software E + Hardware D''		Y	Transvactional Horizontal / Solution upselling
Move 5	Vertical / Segment Move	6	Service C + Software B + Hardware A + Software E + Hardware D''+ Software F	Y		Recurrent Vertical / Segment upselling

IoT^4 Strategic Methodology – canvas #3.2 – Business Models (detailed) per strategic move (output of step 3).

STEP 4: FROM CUSTOMER EXPERIENCE TO DIGITAL SAVVY ORGANIZATIONS

As stated before we are solving the following questions typically asked by CEOs and senior leaders:

- As I have an extended analog portfolio of products (software, hardware) and associated service, what are the elements of my core offerings and my extended portfolio that I will need to adapt to leverage what the IoT holds?
- I understand the need of open architectures and designs to leverage the IoT's ecosystems; but how does this apply to my set of products that I sell as an all-in-one system?
- There seem to be a lot of different standards: how does my core offer fit into that?
- I fear the commoditization due to the need to be open and compatible with numerous third parties: what strategies can we put in place to beat commoditization and competitors?
- Should I look at new business models? If so, how does it fit with my current portfolio and go to market? What strategies can I put in place to leverage those new business models without putting my core business at risk?

Step 4 is making sure that your moves are delivering a portion of your intended customer experience and associate value propositions. Being able to close the loop between the outputs of the methodology and the start point (step 0) is an important milestone; it avoids being focusing on the technology and the business model instead of focusing on what they deliver as an added value to your customers.

Each individual move should be equal to a customer value proposition / gain. The sum of all moves should form together the targeted customer experience.

STEP 4:
From customer experience
to digital savvy organizations

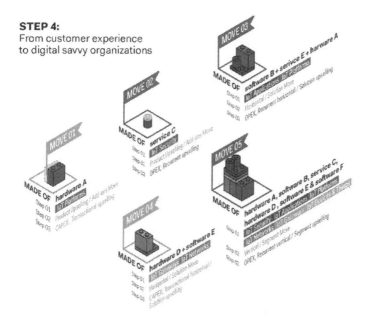

You must make sure that once you have put all your IoT components together (hardware, software and services) for a specific move, that once you have clarified which differentiation strategy and business model best apply, that the overall sum answers specific customer needs. Once the moves and proof of concepts have been validated, comes the execution. Execution needs to be fine-tuned for each organization, each market, competitive landscape and so forth. Our objective is to highlight the importance of having a portfolio strategy but to also consider when defining the execution plan, some important ingredients such as leadership & people and digital savvy organizations.

But don't be misled, defining an IoT portfolio strategy is an important step into digitalization, but nothing can be accomplished without strong leadership and a digital savvy organization.

In chapter 1 and 6, we highlight how a poorly executed good strategy can end up with social disasters. The difficulty and success very often resides in the execution. There is no magic trick and there are plenty of amazing books that will go through the recipes of successful execution.

MORE EXAMPLES:

Note for readers: I will be posting and gathering through my website, www.nicolaswindpassinger.com, more examples on how to use the methodology and how it is being used. Like every methodology, it will evolve. Please share with the community your experience and how we, as a community, can improve it to enable even more IoT successes into delivering unique customer experience and helping analog companies "digitize to profitize".

CHAPTER 10

RECOMMENDATIONS
EXECUTIVE SUMMARY

"The speed of disruption is getting brutal. We say we have to reinvent ourselves every three years. You have to anticipate getting the market transitions right. You have to have the courage for you and your leaders to dramatically change. We've changed more in the last year than we have in any five years before. When you disrupt yourself it's painful and you usually get penalized by the marketplace. But if you don't disrupt yourself, you get put out of business."
John Chambers, Cisco CEO, World Economic Forum in Davos

DIGITIZATION AND FINANCIAL PERFORMANCE ARE TIGHTLY LINKED

Two studies demonstrate the relationship between financial performance, customer satisfaction and digital maturity:

Cap Gemini in their report *The Digital Advantage: How digital leaders outperform their peers in every industry* (5) did surveys on 391 companies and analyzed 184 publicly traded companies to assess their digital maturity and more importantly, link it with their industry adjusted financial performance. The study shows that the companies that combine both investments in technology-enabled initiatives and the needed leadership capabilities outperform their peers. They statistically derive more revenue (+9%), are more profitable (+26%) and have an overall higher market value (+12%).

Another study done by The Path to Digital Transformation (18) shows that a company needs 4 years before digital transformation benefits can be seen financially. The study also highlights that after commencing with a digital transformation program, you get an average of 86% net promoter score by your customers.

On the other side not doing anything about digital transformation is a high-risk option with significant consequences. As stated by Pierre Nanterme (CEO Accenture), "digital is the main reason just over half of the companies on the Fortune 500 have disappeared since the year 2000 (132)" or, John Chambers (Executive Chairman, Cisco System): "At least 40% of all businesses will die in the next 10 years, if they don't figure out how to change their entire company to accommodate new technologies (12)".

INTERNET OF THINGS

Evolution or Revolution?

IoT is the rebranding of the existing Machine to Machine (M2M) market that exists today. IoT will enable horizontal and vertical system architectures as well as create new rules around reliability, robustness, cost, simplicity of usage, set of features, maintenance, integration capabilities, etc. At the same time, it will address and solve end-to-end performance, availability and traceability in a more open and cost-effective way.

Even though the Internet of Things is an important catalyst of digital transformation, it will not, on its own, transform our world. IoT is a milestone amongst other milestones such as virtualization, connectivity, mobility, IP Convergence, Telephony Over IP, and Video Over IP and the result is a more digitalized society.

What makes the IoT different from previous tech evolutions is the fact that it will create the conditions to unleash the huge amount of data that has been inaccessible, due to more connected products, services and customers. It will then enable more intelligence in and outside of the products and environments that surrounds us.

Connectivity will not be the end purpose, connecting things holds very low value by itself; it's the data that is generated by this connectivity that will be tomorrow's gold mine. As things get more and more connected, the need and value of information will exponentially grow. Historical and live stream of raw data will become more valuable over time. More organizations will be selling and buying information from sources that will be able to serve them. Unleashing data, connecting everyone and everything in a seamless network and creating knowledge and value around this uninterrupted flow of information will create the landscape for the next digital milestones that have already started to occur, including:

- Augmented reality,
- Virtual Reality,
- Predictive Analytics,
- Artificial Intelligence and Deep Learning.

When you add reductions in cost to the exponential advances in technologies such as communication and mobility, cloud storage and computing, miniaturization, graphical processing capabilities and robotics, you understand that there will be a switch of value from hardware to software, from software to data stream and from big data to recurrent services.

This will bring commoditization challenges for today's analog manufacturers which must prepare their strategic move to understand how the IoT changes the rules of the game and how it can be leveraged to their benefit to leapfrog their competitors.

Leverage the IoT to Prosper in the Digital Age

Over the years, traditional analog companies have succeeded by developing their organizations, products, staffing, channels, pricing models and so forth using rules which worked well in an analog marketplace. Some of these companies became major, multinational corporations using these business models and operations.

In the new paradigm of IoT, the once successful analog business models and processes are obstructing progress. They are becoming burdensome to the point of threatening the speed of organization are adapting to the new paradigm.

The old analog business models are now a weakness and to survive businesses must adapt.

What has made those analog companies successful is now their biggest weakness. The old ways of thinking and the processes that have worked for decades are quickly being superseded by the digital evolution.

You must understand that IoT's digital transformation can be a unique opportunity to leap frog your competition or to get, on the other side, commoditized and reduced financial performance.

FALSE BELIEFS

You need to be the first one to succeed

There is a common belief that the first is the one that takes it all. The facts show a different reality; timing is indeed the number one success factor (109), but pioneers, on average, lose their leadership in less than 12 years leap frogged by later entrants (31).

The first entrant to the market has paid a high price in research, development and marketing. Latecomers benefit from this by improving the business model, technologies and so forth.

You could liken this to the story of the tortoise and the hare. The hare gets ahead in the race quickly, but the tortoise wins.

You need to be a digital start-up to succeed

Another common belief is that start-ups have all the cards in their hands to beat the well-established analog companies. In fact, analog companies have great weapons to fight back with and even lead the digital transformation, especially if they leverage their considerable resources to fight off the attacks.

When you add those two elements – time and assets - it's not too late for incumbents/analog companies to adapt; they in fact have what is needed to lead and beat competition by leveraging and adapting to the new rules of the game.

THE IMPORTANCE OF CHOOSING A DIGITIZATION STRATEGY

Spend the time to gain an understanding of what is happening, what is preparing to threaten your traditional marketplace and how you, as a leader or as an employee, can leverage those changes for your company's benefit. Make no mistake about it that young, upstart companies are certainly eyeing the historical "analog" channels and markets, sizing them up, and developing new products, services, procedures, channels and paradigms to crack the code and change the rules of the game for their own benefit. But at the same time, as stated in the previous section, traditional analog companies have considerable resources to fight back.

The fact is that IoT changes the rules of the game. The disruptive business models adopted by Airbnb and Uber illustrate how severe the impact a digitization approach can have on well established, analog, market shares.

Manufacturers will need to be nimble, willing and able to pivot hard as this technological evolution progresses. Changes will occur quickly, both in technology and the marketplace, and the tastes and desires of consumers can change without warning.

When studying companies that have tackled change and market disruption in the last decade, data shows that there are in fact four possible strategies available.

- Option #1 - Ignore
- Option #2 - Milk the cow
- Option #3 - U-turn the mothership
- Option #4 - Transforming from the edge

Incumbents will need to transform themselves into digital enterprises if they want to survive. Getting digital is not about investing in the latest technologies; rather, it is about setting up a strategy with the proper timing and dedicating the proper digital capabilities (people, business plans, operations, etc.) to execute upon this same strategy.

The best option from the list above is #4, which is to maintain your existing markets and channels – keep the mothership afloat – while investing money into creating a new opportunity at the edge of your core offer. You could liken this to an organ transplant – keep the body alive while you change out the other parts for newer and more modern parts.

DIGITAL TRANSFORMATION STRATEGY: TRANSFORMING FROM THE EDGE

As stated by Alan Lewis and Dan McKone's in their book *Edge Strategy: A new mindset for profitable growth* (41) : Edge strategies are less risky and can bring higher return than many other options when a company needs to grow their revenue and associate profits. This is achieved by the fact that the risk is often mitigated from elsewhere in the organization and that the aim of such strategies is to harvest more value from existing assets by stepping out into a space that is not well understood by the companies' employees and overall organization.

Edging strategies also contribute to financial performance. Later in "Edge Strategy: A new mindset for profitable growth," Lewis and McKone explain, "Edge achievers have increased risk-adjusted shareholder returns by more than 15 percent versus their peers. Furthermore, these companies have outgrown their peers by 39 percent (42)".

Transforming from the edge requires retraining and/or reallocating resources (people, products, manufacturing capabilities, supply chain capabilities, etc.) and modifying the organization. This approach is difficult, but it takes advantage of the strengths of both the new and the old channels and technology at the same time.

If you want to tap into the IoT opportunity and your company is an established analog player, then this strategy has some real interest as it brings with it great values and it enables you to mix your analog and the digital opportunities into a unique environment in which your analog specificities (intellectual property, customer base, unique value proposition) can make you leap frog all of newcomers that must shoulder the costs to assemble the same assets.

There is no doubt that the IoT is complex in the technologies that compose it, in its standards, in its ecosystems and business models. Applying a "transform from the edge" strategy to a traditional analog company to move their current offer into the IoT space while at the same time avoiding commoditization is not an easy task.

FOUR STEPS TO DIGITIZATION: IOT[4] STRATEGIC METHODOLOGY

What are we trying to solve with the IOT[4] Strategic Methodology? The objective of the methodology is to provide a series of simple and elegant steps to companies looking for digital transformation strategic orientations about their core analog offerings. It's a practical method to "transform from the edge" with a step by step approach.

The methodology is based on four simple steps to make your analog portfolio transition to an IoT compatible portfolio while at the same time avoiding commoditization.

The steps are:

- Start point (Step 0): your customers
- Step 1: making your analog portfolio IoT compatible
- Step 2: defining an offering differentiation strategy to avoid commoditization
- Step 3: choosing the most relevant business models
- Step 4: closing the loop: from customer experience to digital savvy organizations

We have put a lot of efforts into detailing each step of the method both from a theoretical perspective (chapters 4 to 8) and a practical perspective (chapter 9).

I will be posting and gathering through my website, www.nicolaswindpassinger.com, more examples on how to use the methodology and how it is being used. Like every methodology, it will evolve. Please share with the community your experience and how we, as a community, can improve it to enable even more IoT successes into delivering unique customer experience and helping analog companies "digitize to profitize".

FROM ANALOG TO DIGITAL SAVVY ORGANIZATIONS

Some companies might strategically choose to milk the cow and ignore the IoT's digital transformation impacts; some others might choose to try to U-turn their companies or even ignore what their company might be facing in the coming years.

If you decide that you want your company to begin leveraging the IoT and leapfrog past your competitors, then you will need to define an IoT strategy maximizing your company's current offer portfolio and resources.

But there are still some missing pieces of the puzzle. You still need to clarify the how; in other words, how will you make it happen? What are the different options?

Thinking that strategizing your digitization moves using the IOT[4] METHODOLOGY is enough is wrong; it's in fact just the beginning.

Senior leadership sponsorship and oversight is needed to digitally transform a customer experience, an existing portfolio and turn an analog savvy organization into a digital savvy organization.

There are five execution strategies when dealing with digital transformation which apply perfectly to the "transforming from the edge" strategic option (6) as reported by a World Economic Forum White Paper:

- Build
- Acquire – Buy
- Partner or Ally
- Invest
- Co-develop

We give great details on each of them in chapter 8. Whatever strategy you decide to choose, there are some important areas to tackle when dealing with transforming your organization into a digital savvy organization. Those areas are:

- Digital leadership & people
- Digital mine canaries
- the importance of the how
- internal communication and story telling
- middle management and innovation
- sense of urgency
- the importance of R & D including failure & improvisation as well as internal hackathons and internal hackers
- the importance of digital diversity across generations and digital talent management
- the importance of your partners , IoT channels and associate partner programs
- the importance of ecosystems and alliances

CONCLUSION

Ode to Digital Mine Canaries

Digitization is a strong contributor to revenue, profitability, employee and customer satisfaction.

Leaders who decide that digitization needs to be a core component of their company's strategy and who align the associate investments, initiatives and leadership not only outperform their peers by revenue and profitability but also increase both customer and employee satisfaction.

IoT is at the forefront of digital transformation.

If you are operating in a traditional analog market, you can be sure that newcomers are actively exploring and developing ways to leverage the IoT in order to make inroads into your markets, regardless of the size of your business, the strength of your sales or the depth of your market penetration.

Even though the IoT is an evolution of the Machine to Machine technologies, it is gaining traction not only thanks to better connectivity and increase of available bandwidth but also through massive cost improvement and globalization of markets.

It is imperative that the leadership within your company assesses and strategizes what the IoT might mean for your business, even at the sake of disrupting it, because if you don't, the competition will. This disruption is coming far more quickly than you think and changes are already fast occurring. You might not even be aware that you are already engaged in a speed race that embraces different aspects of digital transformation: technology, go to market, innovation, organizations and ecosystems.

The Internet of Things is at its inflection point.

The rules of the games in business, which have applied for decades and established the current enterprise landscape, are changing fast. IoT will disrupt leading businesses, the choice is yours to use this transformation to your benefit. There is a short time window of opportunity when technologies evolve but have not established their "rules of the game". This is what happened to digital cameras in the 90s; this is what happened with the internet in the beginning of 2000, this is what is happening to the IoT right now. Now is a unique opportunity to change and adapt the rules of the game to outperform your competitors.

What the IoT brings to the table is unique in that it changes the rules of the game for traditional analog companies which at the same time creates the conditions for newcomers to have a bigger piece of the pie without paying the high entry fees. Analog players have considerable resources to fight off the attacks including investment capitals, strong brands, strong channels and influence power on standardization, market price, specifiers, etc.

IoT without a doubt will disrupt industries, ecosystems and organizations.

Some organizations will decide to transform their traditional analog company from the edge, while some others might decide not to do anything and just milk the cow.

The IoT will connect not only things with things, people with things, and people with people but will unleash a flow of data that has never been experienced, until now. Owning the source of data, building value from it and improving the business relevancy of your offers to the end user will be among the game changers. The game will be less about selling products than owning the relationship and the data. Tomorrow's winners will be the ones that have managed not only to connect their customers but those who have made sense of the consequential flow of data to the end user.

IoT is a digitization milestone of our society.

Digital transformation has been happening for more than 20 years; the IoT is one among other milestones of the digitization of our society and economy; but this will create the conditions to the next digital transformation including virtual reality, analytics, artificial intelligence and deep knowledge.

Blockchain will unlock the IoT promises.

Blockchain will be a key accelerator of the IoT evolution. Its impact will spread among all industries and usages. Blockchain technologies are an answer to the main roadblocks to an exponential growth of connected things: trust, ownership and record. It will disrupt not only banking ecosystem and associated financial transactions, but will open the door to a series of IoT usages/applications that will create tomorrow's unicorns.

Digitization starts with customers.

Digitization is an enabler to better serve and bring more value to your current and future customers. If you are obsessed to solve problems for your customers, to help them in their everyday operations and bring a strong contribution to their business; IoT will be an incredible opportunity for your business. Investigate what is desired and needed by your customers. Understand what the IoT is and will bring. Innovate and do not hesitate to disrupt your organization from the edge.

Showing and demonstrating a customer-centric culture and approach is the compass that guides the organization towards a successful digital transformation, leveraging both the risks and the opportunities to leapfrog the competition.

Raw flow of data and connecting customers' assets is critical for your future.

The difference between just selling hardware or using the data and connecting the customer's assets is the difference between making a single sale and receiving a recurrent, predictable flow of money.

The rawer the data you collect from your end user, the more you can build knowledge and deliver better value. Connecting assets and leveraging the resulting flow of data to build unique advanced software services such as analytics will not only drive end user satisfaction but also accelerate their overall financial performance. Not only does this bring more recurring revenue but it also enables the companies to have a more in-depth, added value relationship with their end-users and therefore be more business relevant for their operations. Being more business relevant enables companies to have a more captive installed base of customers, avoid commoditization and enhance end user satisfaction.

Digitize or Die.

Take the risk to be at the forefront of digital transformation.

Transform the risk into an opportunity.

Don't be afraid of being that Digital Mine Canary. Recognize and act upon the urgency before it's too late.

Thank you:

I'm grateful that you have taken time out of your busy schedules to read this book. I sincerely hope the contents of this book have helped you understand what IoT means for you, and that the knowledge I shared will help you in your digitization journey.

I encourage you therefore to hack this book to your full digital advantage. Create the leading-edge future. Educate your team members. Develop and truly maximize digitization within your own enterprise and ultimately succeed and 'profitize'.

Perhaps our paths will cross, and I will have the privilege of hearing that this book has helped you in your professional and personal life journey. I will be posting and gathering through my website, www.nicolaswindpassinger.com, more examples on how to use the methodology and how it is being used. Like every methodology, it will evolve. Please share with the community your experience and how we, as a community, can improve it to enable even more IoT successes into delivering unique customer experience and helping analog company "digitize to profitize".

It starts and ends with what **you** are going to do when you close this book.

PERSPECTIVE

During the research of this book, I reached out specifically to Don Tapscott and Olivier Hersent to get their perspective of where the IoT was heading. Each one provided their views which I have included for you to read.

Digitize or Unplug

Digitize or Die is not a technology book, it is an explanation about the profound impact of the acceleration of time in our world, and how to rethink the way we work, build products or companies in this context.

If you are not convinced that we are living through an unprecedented era of change, then the first chapters of the book will provide striking examples of the acceleration of innovation cycles in the last century. Yuval Noah Harari, in his book "Sapiens", goes back even further in the history of mankind and demonstrates that humans have never been exposed to such a magnitude of change during the span of one's life. Life on earth is designed to adapt to changes spanning thousands of years at best, not decades or even years. There is a fundamental question whether our body can sustain such a stress -and for how much longer- as innovation keeps accelerating.

While this is an interesting problem for philosophers and sociologists who can afford to step back from the world and analyze it, CxOs do not have this luxury. The changes of our world are a fact, and for any company there is no way to ignore them... denial is synonymous with death in the business world.

So, we need to change and work differently. But what kind of change?

We need to go "digital". Of course, "digital" is one of these buzzwords that epitomizes the common denominator of many different transformations. This book explores many facets of "digitization", which applies to customer relations, to product development, and to the industry in general.

As we humans live through accelerated change and increasing stress, somehow we tend to transfer this stress into our own actions and desires. We need to get what we want faster and faster. Our own desire for immediacy fuels the spiral of accelerating change. Twenty years ago, we would happily order a book from a local bookstore and receive it a week later. Today we find it almost unbearable not to receive the book overnight. It becomes even scarier when you realize that in many cases the human factor has become an obstacle already: you actually WANT to just type a title and click "buy", you don't want to walk to the bookstore, you don't even want to make a phone call, you just want to "click".

Digitization is essentially this: pervasive immediacy and de-intermediation in all domains, APIs everywhere. The Internet of Things is just one facet of this: by decreasing the cost of turning anything into a connected thing, the IoT pushes the frontier of the digital world.

The digital, connected, immediate world brings many benefits. For example, "large numbers" are not frightening anymore. The electric grid is a perfect example. In the past utilities considered end users as a "large mass" that could be modelled statistically, but could not be addressed individually. There was nothing smart to do with end-users, they were just a passive "mass". In the digital world, this is no longer true. In the next 10 years, all our boilers, radiators, HVACs, electric cars, but also all large electricity users around us will adapt their power consumption instantly, and automatically, to the varying production of ever increasing solar & renewable energy. Something that was considered nonsense ten years ago is now easy and natural with IoT networks such as Low Power Wide Area Networks (LPWANs).

The "digital" version of our world, re-created through an ever-increasing number of sensors, makes it <u>directly</u> accessible to mathematicians and universities all over the world. We are used to a relatively slow, intermediated, innovation path from the new math discovery to applied R&D to products. Expect another acceleration of change as the digital world de-intermediates anyone between the mathematician and the real world. We are about to see the sheer power of advanced science in action, optimizing our world in ways that will instantly obsolete many traditional practices.

It is true that the economy, and our own nature, urges us and our businesses to keep up with the innovation race and become digital, contributing to the spiral of exponential change. But still this is a world for humans, and I believe we are approaching the limits of how fast humans can spin in the innovation spiral. Many of us will need to step back, we will need to learn how to re-introduce time as a necessary dimension of our human nature... we need to find ways to innovate without becoming a prisoner of the innovation hurricane. The urge for innovation will create an equally powerful urge to step aside and become humans and philosophers again. There will be profitable businesses that will concentrate on human beings rather than innovation.

Digitize or .... unplug?

Olivier Hersent is the Chairman & Chief Technology Officer at Actility

THE LEDGER OF THINGS

As this helpful book explains, the physical world is being animated -- becoming smart and interconnected. Billions soon trillions of inert objects becoming intelligent and communicating devices. These devices will not just sense and communicate they will conduct transactions and participate in the economy. To do so they must trust each other and establish their reputations as trustworthy.

Such value creating commercial activities will not go through something like the VISA network. It will require a distributed ledger. The Internet of Things needs a Ledger of Things.

So it turns out that Blockchain, the powerful new technology that underpins cryptocurrencies like Bitcoin, is critical to this. Blockchain is a vast, global distributed ledger or database running on millions of devices and open to anyone, where not just information but anything of *value* – like money and units of energy - can be moved and stored securely and privately peer to peer, and where trust is established, not by powerful intermediaries like banks, governments and technology companies, but rather through mass collaboration and clever code.

Blockchain technology enables trust and secure storage, as well as movement of transactional and other data between those things. Add in Artificial Intelligence so that these devises can learn and become capable of doing things that they weren't initially programmed to do and we can see the contours of the animated physical world.

Take the power grid for example, by using emerging software and technologies, we can instill intelligence into existing infrastructure by adding smart devices that can communicate with one another, and reconfigure themselves depending upon availability of bandwidth, storage, or other capacity, and therefore resist interruption.

When my son and I were writing *Blockchain Revolution* our objective was to explain how the technology behind Bitcoin will change the world as we know it today. As we dug into the issues we realized that this technology would not just underpin transactions between people but also transactions between things. A new world is emerging where things can learn to trust each other, collaborate, and create value at the command of humans. The Ledger of Things keeps track of everything including reputation of devices to be trustworthy.

There are potential applications across virtually every sector: Transportation, Infrastructure, Energy, waste, and water management, Resource extraction and farming, Financial services and insurance, Real estate management, Industrial operations and Retail.

We can shape these markets per our values—as individuals, companies, and societies—and code these values into the Blockchain, such as incentives to use renewable energy, honor price commitments, and protect privacy. In short, the Ledger of Things, on top of the IoT, animates and personalizes the physical world even as we share more.

The questions managers, entrepreneurs, and civic leaders need to ask are: How will we take advantage of these new opportunities to change and grow? How will our organization respond to the inevitable disruption to our existing operational model? How will we compete with the creative new models of start-ups and collaborations?

In fact, the answer is the starting point of your journey: education. Read about Blockchain and Artificial Intelligence as they will change the world. Your next step is in fact a couple of pages ahead; turn them to understand the IoT rules of the game and learn how to use them to your benefit.

Don Tapscott is the author of 15 widely read books about technology in business and society, including The Digital Economy, Growing Up Digital, and Wikinomics as well as his latest book Blockchain Revolution: How the Technology Behind Bitcoin is Changing Money, Business and the World. He is the CEO of the Tapscott Group and ranked by Thinkers 50 as the 4th most important living business thinker in the world.

REFERENCES

1. Rifkin, Jeremy. The Third Industrial Revolution. *The Third Industrial Revolution.* [Online] http://www.thethirdindustrialrevolution.com/.

2. Lauchlan, Stuart. World Economic Forum – dealing with the new digital context. *Diginomica.* [Online] January 22, 2015. http://diginomica.com/2015/01/22/world-economic-forum-dealing-new-digital-context/.

3. *The DIGITAL UNIVERSE of OPPORTUNITIES.* s.l. : EMC, 2014. p. 17.

4. MacGillivray, Carrie. *IDC FutureScape: Worldwide Internet of Things 2016 Predictions.* s.l. : IDC Research, Inc., 2016.

5. How Digital Leaders Outperform their Peers in Every Industry. *Capgemini Consulting.* [Online] November 5, 2002. https://www.capgemini.com/resources/the-digital-advantage-how-digital-leaders-outperform-their-peers-in-every-industry.

6. Lee, Aileen. Welcome To The Unicorn Club: Learning From Billion-Dollar Startups. *TechCrunch.* [Online] November 2, 2013. https://techcrunch.com/2013/11/02/welcome-to-the-unicorn-club/.

7. McKineey, Phil. Killer Innovations. *http://killerinnovations.com/5-innovation-blind-spots-that-killed-nokia-and-kodak-s11-ep9/.* [Online] http://killerinnovations.com/5-innovation-blind-spots-that-killed-nokia-and-kodak-s11-ep9/.

8. *The World Economic White Paper, Digital transformation of industries.* 2016. p. 4.

9. Internet of Things Global Standards Initiative. *ITU news.* [Online] July 2015. https://itunews.itu.int/En/4291-The-Internet-of-things-Machines-businesses-people-everything-.note.aspx.

10. *Machine-to-Machine communications (M2M); Definitions.* s.l. : ETSI, 2013. p. 9.

11. *The Industrial Internet of Things.* s.l. : National Instruments.

12. Why 40 Percent of Businesses Will Die in the Next 10 Years. *RossRoss.Com.* [Online] October 6, 2016. http://www.rossross.com/blog/40-percent-of-businesses-today-will-die-in-10-years.

13. Solis, Brian. *The End of Business As Usual: Rewire the Way You Work to Succeed in the Consumer Revolution.* s.l. : Wiley, 2011. 1118077555.

14. Half of the world's banks set to fall by the digital wayside - BBVA. *BBVA.* [Online] February 2015, 2015. https://www.finextra.com/news/fullstory.aspx?newsitemid=26965.

15. Francisco González shares BBVA's digital transformation case with Harvard Business School faculty. *BBVA.* [Online] November 21, 2015. https://www.bbva.com/en/news/science-technology/technologies/francisco-gonzalez-shares-bbvas-digital-transformation-case-with-harvard-business-school-faculty-2/.

16. Microsoft to acquire Nokia's devices & services business, license Nokia's patents and mapping services. [Online] September 3, 2013. https://news.microsoft.com/2013/09/03/microsoft-to-acquire-nokias-devices-services-business-license-nokias-patents-and-mapping-services/.

17. Williams, Jeff. Survey says... Windows 10 is highly regarded and very well liked. *TweakTown.* [Online] January 10, 2016. http://www.tweaktown.com/news/49685/survey-windows-10-highly-regarded-very-liked/index.html.

18. Sector Theme & Trends. [Online] http://thepathtodigitaltransformation.com/themes-trends/.

19. Gartner Survey Finds That Two-Fifths of IT Professionals Consider Their IT Organisation Ready for Digital Business. [Online] July 13, 2016. http://www.gartner.com/newsroom/id/3375817.

20. The Internet of Things: Mapping the Value Beyond the Hype. [Online] June 2015.

https://www.mckinsey.de/files/unlocking_the_potential_of_the_intern et_of_things_full_report.pdf.

21. Frederic Dalsace, Wolfgang Ulaga and Chloé Renault. *Michelin Fleet Solutions", HEC Case Study N° HEC-M17L.* 2015.

22. Global market share held by leading smartphone vendors from 4th quarter 2009 to 3rd quarter 2016. [Online] [Cited: 05 06, 2017.] https://www.statista.com/statistics/271496/global-market-share-held-by-smartphone-vendors-since-4th-quarter-2009/.

23. Cheng, Roger. Farewell Nokia: The rise and fall of a mobile pioneer. *CNET.* [Online] April 25, 2014. https://www.cnet.com/news/farewell-nokia-the-rise-and-fall-of-a-mobile-pioneer/.

24. Ericsson Mobility Report June 2016. [Online] June 2016. https://www.ericsson.com/res/docs/2016/ericsson-mobility-report-2016.pdf.

25. Team, Telefónica IoT. 16 Facts you should know about the IoT in 2016. [Online] January 29, 2016. https://iot.telefonica.com/blog/16-facts-you-should-know-about-the-iot-in-2016.

26. Staff, Equities. Eastman Kodak Company Common New (KODK) Plunges 9.91% on November 18. [Online] November 18, 2016. https://www.equities.com/news/eastman-kodak-company-common-new-kodk-plunges-9-91-on-november-18.

27. Antoine Gara, Joe Deaux. Kodak's Bankruptcy: Manufacturing a 21st Century Rebirth. [Online] August 1, 2013. https://www.thestreet.com/story/11995806/1/kodaks-bankruptcy-manufacturing-a-21st-century-rebirth.html.

28. Deutsch, Claudia H. Chief Says Kodak Is Pointed in the Right Direction. [Online] December 25, 1999. http://www.nytimes.com/1999/12/25/business/chief-says-kodak-is-pointed-in-the-right-direction.html.

29. Anthony, Scott. Kodak's Downfall Wasn't About Technology. [Online] July 15, 2016. https://hbr.org/2016/07/kodaks-downfall-wasnt-about-technology.

30. Gartner Says 6.4 Billion Connected "Things" Will Be in Use in 2016, Up 30 Percent From 2015. *Gartner.* [Online] November 10, 2015. http://www.gartner.com/newsroom/id/3165317.

31. Golder, Gerard J. Tellis and Peter N. *Pioneer Advantage: Marketing Logic or Marketing Legend?* s.l. : Journal of Marketing Research, 1993. p. 169.

32. Schwab, Klaus. Are you ready for the technological revolution? *World Economic Forum.* [Online] February 19, 2015. https://www.weforum.org/agenda/2015/02/are-you-ready-for-the-technological-revolution/.

33. Open Source Robotics Foundation. [Online] http://www.osrfoundation.org/osrf-projects/).

34. The DARPA Grand Challenge: Ten Years Later. *DARPA.* [Online] March 13, 2014. http://www.darpa.mil/news-events/2014-03-13.

35. *IoT Megatrends 2016: Six key trends in the IoT developer economy.* s.l. : Vision Mobile. p. 42.

36. *IoT Megatrends 2016: Six key trends in the IoT developer economy.* s.l. : Vision Mobile, 2015. p. 15.

37. Didier Bonnet, Jerome Buvat and Subrahmanyam KVJ. *Monetizing the Internet of Things: Extracting Value from the Connectivity Opportunity.* s.l. : Capgemini Consulting, 2014. p. 8.

38. —. *Monetizing the Internet of Things: Extracting Value from the Connectivity Opportunity.* 2014. p. 4.

39. Resnick, Craig. *GE's Industrial Internet of Things Journey.* s.l. : ARC View, 2016. p. 4.

40. Winig, Laura. GE'S Big Bet on Data and Analytics. [Online] February 18, 2016. http://sloanreview.mit.edu/case-study/ge-big-bet-on-data-and-analytics/.

41. McKone, Alan Lewis and Dan. *Edge Strategy: A new mindset for profitable growth.* s.l. : Harvard Business Review. p. 11.

42. —. *Edge Strategy: A new mindset for profitable growth.* p. 16.

43. Kawasaki, Guy. *Enchantment: The Art of Changing Hearts, Minds, and Actions.* s.l. : Portfolio, 2012. 978-1591845836.

44. Alan Smith, Alexander Osterwalder, Greg Bernarda, Gregory Bernarda, Trish Papadakos, and Yves Pigneur. *Value Proposition Design: How to Create Products and Services Customers Want.* s.l. : Wiley, 2015.

45. Kurzwell, Ray. The Law of Accelerating Returns. *Kurzwell Accelerating Intelligence.* [Online] March 7, 2001. http://www.kurzweilai.net/the-law-of-accelerating-returns.

46. Bob Briscoe, Andrew Odlyzko and Benjamin Tilly. Metcalfe's Law is Wrong. *IEEE Spectrum.* [Online] July 1, 2006. http://spectrum.ieee.org/computing/networks/metcalfes-law-is-wrong.

47. Gilder, George. *Telecosm: How Infinite Bandwidth Will Revolutionize Our World.* s.l. : Simon and Schuster Digital Sales Inc, 2000.

48. Jonathan G. Koomey, Stephen Berard, Marla Sanchez, Henry Wong. *Assessing Trends in the Electrical Efficiency of Computation Over Time.* 2009.

49. *Position Paper on Standardization for IoT technologies.* IERC. 2015.

50. Information technology -- Open Systems Interconnection -- Basic Reference Model: The Basic Mode. *International Standards, ISO/IEC 7498-1:1994, second edition 1994-11-15.* [Online] 1994. http://standards.iso.org/ittf/PubliclyAvailableStandards/s020269_ISO_IEC_7498-1_1994(E).zip.

51. Force, Internet Engineering Task. Requirements for Internet Hosts. Communication Layers. [Online] October 1989. https://tools.ietf.org/html/rfc1122.

52. —. Requirements for Internet Hosts. Application and Support. [Online] October 1989. https://tools.ietf.org/html/rfc1123.

53. Chaouchi, Hakima. *The Internet of Things: Connecting Objects.* s.l. : John Wiley & Sons, 2010.

54. IPv6 for IoT. [Online] IoT6.eu, 2014. [Cited: 01 26, 2017.] http://iot6.eu/ipv6_for_iot.

55. IPv6 Enabled WWW Web Sites List. [Online] IPv6 Forum, 2009. http://www.ipv6forum.com/ipv6_enabled/approval_list.php.

56. IoT6.eu - Researching IPv6 potential for the Internet of Things. [Online] http://iot6.eu/.

57. IEEE. IEEE - The World's largest professional organization for the advancement of technology - IEEE at a glance. [Online] IEEE. http://www.ieee.org/about/today/at_a_glance.html.

58. IETF. The Internet Engineering Task Force (IETF®). [Online] https://www.ietf.org/.

59. OASIS: Advancing open standards for the information society. [Online] https://www.oasis-open.org/.

60. iot6.eu. IPv6 advantages for IoT. [Online] http://iot6.eu/ipv6_advantages_for_iot.

61. IoT6.eu. IoT6 architecture. [Online] IoT6. http://iot6.eu/iot6_architecture.

62. IEEE 802.15 Working Group for Wireless Specialty Networks (WSN). [Online] http://www.ieee802.org/15/about.html.

63. IEEE 802.15 WPAN™ Task Group 4 (TG4). [Online] http://www.ieee802.org/15/pub/TG4.html.

64. IPv6 for IoT. [Online] http://iot6.eu/ipv6_for_iot.

65. Transmission of IPv6 Packets over IEEE 802.15.4 Networks. [Online] https://tools.ietf.org/html/rfc4944.

66. RPL: IPv6 Routing Protocol for Low-Power and Lossy Networks. [Online] https://tools.ietf.org/html/rfc6550.

67. Group Communication for the Constrained Application Protocol (CoAP). [Online] https://tools.ietf.org/html/rfc7390.

68. MQTT Version 3.1.1 OASIS Standard. [Online] October 29, 2014. http://docs.oasis-open.org/mqtt/mqtt/v3.1.1/os/mqtt-v3.1.1-os.html.

69. Extensible Messaging and Presence Protocol (XMPP): Core. [Online] https://tools.ietf.org/html/rfc3920.

70. ISO/IEC 19464:2014 - Information technology -- Advanced Message Queuing Protocol (AMQP) v1.0 specification. [Online] 2014. http://www.iso.org/iso/home/store/catalogue_tc/catalogue_detail.htm?csnumber=64955.

71. IEEE Conformity Assessment Program (ICAP). [Online] http://standards.ieee.org/faqs/icap.html.

72. WiFi Certification. [Online] https://www.wi-fi.org/certification.

73. littleBits. [Online] http://www.littlebits.cc.

74. Morrish, Jim. The Emergence of M2M/IoT Application Platforms. *Machina Research White Paper.* [Online] September 2013. https://machinaresearch.com/static/media/uploads/Machina%20Research%20White%20Paper%20-%20M2M_IoT%20Application%20Platforms.pdf.

75. Perard, Luc. Are you confused about IoT platforms? [Online] August 24, 2015. https://www.linkedin.com/pulse/you-confused-iot-platforms-luc-perard.

76. —. The IoT Apps That Wanted To Be A Platform. [Online] November 12, 2015. https://www.linkedin.com/pulse/iot-apps-wanted-platform-luc-perard?trk=mp-reader-card.

77. Android Things: Build connected devices for a wide variety of consumer, retail, and industrial applications. [Online] https://developer.android.com/things/index.html.

78. Weave. [Online] https://developers.google.com/weave/.

79. NFC. NFC Forum. [Online] http://nfc-forum.org.

80. NEARFIELDCOMMUNICATIONNFC.NET. NFC versus Bluetooth. [Online] 2017. [Cited: 01 27, 2017.] http://www.nearfieldcommunicationnfc.net/nfc-vs-bluetooth.html.

81. SIG, Bluetooth. Bluetooth Core Specification. [Online] 2017. [Cited: 01 27, 2017.] https://www.bluetooth.com/specifications/bluetooth-core-specification.

82. Group, Thread. *Thread Stack Fundamentals.* s.l. : Thread Group, July 2015. White paper.

83. Daintree Networks Inc. *Applying Mesh Networking.* s.l. : Daintree Networks Inc. White Paper.

84. ZigBee Alliance. ZigBee Home Automation. [Online] ZigBee . [Cited: 01 27, 2017.] http://www.zigbee.org/zigbee-for-developers/applicationstandards/zigbeehomeautomation/.

85. Z-Wave Alliance. Z-Wave Alliance: Our History. [Online] [Cited: 01 27, 2017.] http://z-wavealliance.org/z-wave_alliance_history.

86. —. Z-Wave: The Basics. [Online] [Cited: 01 27, 2017.] http://www.z-wave.com/faq.

87. EnOcean Alliance. EnOcean Wireless Standard ISO/IEC 14543-3-10. [Online] https://www.enocean-alliance.org/en/enocean_standard/.

88. Wi-Fi Alliance. Wi-Fi Alliance: The worldwide network of companies. [Online] [Cited: 01 28, 2017.] https://www.wi-fi.org/.

89. Wi-Fi Alliance®. Wi-Fi Alliance® introduces low power, long range Wi-Fi HaLow™. [Online] 01 04, 2016. [Cited: 01 28, 2017.] https://www.wi-fi.org/news-events/newsroom/wi-fi-alliance-introduces-low-power-long-range-wi-fi-halow.

90. DASH7 Alliance . DASH7 Alliance. [Online] [Cited: 01 28, 2017.] http://www.dash7-alliance.org/.

91. Wi-SUN Alliance. [Online] https://www.wi-sun.org/index.php/en/.

92. ZigBee Alliance. JupiterMesh® Neighborhood Area Network (NAN) Announced. [Online] 06 08, 2016. [Cited: 01 29, 2017.] http://www.zigbee.org/jupitermesh-neighborhood-area-network-nan-announced.

93. Sigfox. [Online] [Cited: 01 28, 2017.] https://www.sigfox.com/fr.

94. LoRa Alliance™. About the LoRa Alliance™. [Online] https://www.lora-alliance.org/The-Alliance/About-the-Alliance.

95. Semtech. [Online] http://www.semtech.com/.

96. ingenu. Ingenu: About US. [Online] http://www.ingenu.com/company/about-us/.

97. Ericsson. *CELLULAR NETWORKS FOR MASSIVE IOT • DELIVERING NEW VALUE IN THE NETWORKED SOCIETY.* s.l. : Ericsson, 2016.

98. Nokia. *LTE evolution for IoT connectivity.* s.l. : Nokia, 2016.

99. Weightless Special Interest Group (SIG). What Is Weightless? [Online] http://www.weightless.org/.

100. Joseph Menn, Jim Finkle and Dustin Volz. Cyber attacks disrupt PayPal, Twitter, other sites. [Online] October 21, 2016. http://www.reuters.com/article/us-usa-cyber-idUSKCN12L1ME.

101. Loshin, Peter. Details emerging on Dyn DNS DDoS attack, Mirai IoT botnet. [Online] Octover 28, 2016. http://searchsecurity.techtarget.com/news/450401962/Details-emerging-on-Dyn-DNS-DDoS-attack-Mirai-IoT-botnet.

102. Ashford, Warwick. Mirai IoT botnet code release raises fears of surge in DDoS attacks. [Online] October 4, 2016. http://www.computerweekly.com/news/450400311/Mirai-IoT-botnet-code-release-raises-fears-of-surge-in-DDoS-attacks.

103. Strother, Neil. IoT and the Future of Networked Energy. [Online] 2016. https://www.navigantresearch.com/research/iot-and-the-future-of-networked-energy.

104. Enders, Tawfik Jelassi and Albrecht. *Strategies for E-business: Creating Value Through Electronic and Mobile commerce.* p. 127.

105. Bower, Clark Gilbert and Joseph L. Disruptive Change: When Trying Harder Is Part of the Problem. [Online] May 2002. https://hbr.org/2002/05/disruptive-change-when-trying-harder-is-part-of-the-problem.

106. Mui, Chanka. How Kodak Failed. [Online] January 18, 2012. http://www.forbes.com/sites/chunkamui/2012/01/18/how-kodak-failed/#1f5215cebd6a.

107. KNC. How Fujifilm survived. [Online] The Economist, 01 18, 2012. [Cited: 02 01, 2017.] http://www.economist.com/blogs/schumpeter/2012/01/how-fujifilm-survived.

108. Gerald C. Kane, Doug Palmer, Anh Nguyen Phillips, David Kiron and Natasha Buckley. Strategy, not Technology, Drives Digital Transformation. [Online] 2015. http://www2.deloitte.com/content/dam/Deloitte/cn/Documents/technology-media-telecommunications/deloitte-cn-tmt-strategy-not-technology-drive-digital-transformation-en-150930.pdf.

109. Gross, Bill. Why clean technology is a trillion-dollar opportunity. [Online] October 11, 2016. https://www.youtube.com/watch?v=ZwSdc70LUpg.

110. McKone, Alan Lewis and Dan. *Edge Strategy: A new mindset for profitable growth.* p. ix.

111. —. *Edge Strategy: A new mindset for profitable growth.* p. 13.

112. Minimum Viable Product. [Online] SyncDev. http://www.syncdev.com/minimum-viable-product/.

113. *The Digital Transformation Agenda 2016.* s.l. : The Economist, 2016. p. 4.

114. Heath, Chip Heath and Dan. *Made to Stick.* s.l. : Random House. p. 253.

115. Tara Swart, Kitty Chisholm and Paul Brown. *Neuroscience for Leadership, 2015 Edition.* s.l. : Palgrave Macmillan, 2015.

116. Rathgeber, Dr. John Kotter and Holger. *That's Not How We Do It Here!: A Story About How Organizations Rise and Fall—and Can Rise Again.* s.l. : Portfolio , 2016.

117. Kotter, John. Misconceptions about Leadership and Management. [Online] LinkedIn, 07 20, 2016. [Cited: 02 04, 2017.] https://www.linkedin.com/pulse/misconceptions-leadership-management-john-kotter.

118. Smith, Andrea Nagy. What was Polaroid thinking? *Yale School of Management.* [Online] November 4, 2009. http://insights.som.yale.edu/insights/what-was-polaroid-thinking.

119. Grant, Adam. *Originals: How Non-conformists Change the World.* s.l. : WH Allen, 2016.

120. Homans, George C. *The Human Group (The International Library of Sociology).* s.l. : Routledge, 2010.

121. Homans, George Caspar. *Social Behavior: Its Elementary Forms.* s.l. : Harcourt Brace, 1974.

122. Huy, Quy Nguyen. In Praise of Middle Managers. *Harvard Business Review.* [Online] September 2001. https://hbr.org/2001/09/in-praise-of-middle-managers).

123. Huy, Quy. What Could Have Saved Nokia, and What Can Other Companies Learn? *Insead Knowledge.* [Online] March 13, 2014. http://knowledge.insead.edu/strategy/what-could-have-saved-nokia-and-what-can-other-companies-learn-3220#9DYQRpvqVUDPte7q.99.

124. Kotter, John. *Leading Change.* 2015.

125. Zimmerman, Eilene. Baba Shiv: Failure is the Mother of Innovation. [Online] 03 02, 2016. [Cited: 02 04, 2017.] https://www.gsb.stanford.edu/insights/baba-shiv-failure-mother-innovation.

126. Jarmoc, Jeff. Tweet. [Online] 10 21, 2016. [Cited: 03 04, 2017.] https://twitter.com/jjarmoc/status/789637654711267328.

127. Indeed. "internet of things" or IoT Job Trends. [Online] [Cited: 03 04, 2017.] https://www.indeed.com/jobtrends/q-%22internet-of-things%22-or-IoT.html?relative=1.

128. IoT Talent. About Us. [Online] 2017. [Cited: 03 04, 2017.] https://www.iottalent.org/about-us.

129. Cisco. The Internet of Things World Forum Unites Industry Leaders in Chicago to Accelerate the Adoption of IoT Business Models. [Online] 10 14, 2014. [Cited: 03 04, 2017.] https://newsroom.cisco.com/press-release-content?articleId=1499853.

130. Steinhilber, Steve. *Strategic Alliances: Three Ways to Make Them Work* . s.l. : Harvard Business Review Press, 2008.

131. Solis, Brian. *X: The Experience When Business Meets Design.* s.l. : Wiley, 2015. 1118456548.

132. Nanterme, Pierre. Digital disruption has only just begun. *World Economic Forum Davos 2016.* [Online] January 17, 2016. https://www.weforum.org/agenda/2016/01/digital-disruption-has-only-just-begun/.

INFOGRAPHICS REFERENCES

IMD and Cisco. 2015. *Digital Vortex: How Digital Disruption Is Redefining Industries.* Global Center for Digital Business Transformation. http://www.cisco.com/c/dam/en/us/solutions/collateral/industry-solutions/digital-vortex-report.pdf.

s.d. http://www.verizonenterprise.com/resources/infographic/ig_som-iot-infographic_en_xg.pdf.

Adam Wright, Carrie MacGillivray, Vernon Turner. 2016. «2015 Global IoT Decision Maker Survey: C-Level Analysis.» *IDC.* 03. Accès le 07 2017. https://www.idc.com/getdoc.jsp?containerId=US41082016.

BI Intelligence . 2016. «Here's how the Internet of Things will explode by 2020.» *Business Insider UK.* 01 09. Accès le 07 2017. http://uk.businessinsider.com/iot-ecosystem-internet-of-things-forecasts-and-business-opportunities-2016-2?r=US&IR=T.

Capgemini Consulting. s.d. «The Digital Advantage: How digital leaders outperform their peers in every industry.» https://www.capgemini.com/resource-file-access/resource/pdf/The_Digital_Advantage__How_Digital_Leaders_Outperform_their_Peers_in_Every_Industry.pdf.

Dávalos, Edilberto Barrero. 2016. «The IoT Market in 2016 - Social, Economic & Business Challenges.» *https://www.slideshare.net.* 17 10. Accès le 07 2017. https://www.slideshare.net/edilbertobarrero/ss-eb31?qid=dce12431-c7f6-4155-837d-5273d79a4b65&v=&b=&from_search=3.

2016. «Digital Enterprise.» *World Economic Forum White Paper.* http://reports.weforum.org/digital-transformation/wp-content/blogs.dir/94/mp/files/pages/files/digital-enterprise-narrative-final-january-2016.pdf.

Forrester. 2016. «Global Business Technographics® Networks And Telecommunications Survey, 2016.» *Forrester.* 03. Accès le 07 2017. https://www.forrester.com/Global+Business+Technographics+Networks+And+Telecommunications+Survey+2016/-/E-sus3011.

GERALD C. KANE, DOUG PALMER, ANH NGUYEN PHILLIPS, DAVID KIRON, AND NATASHA BUCKLEY. 2016. «ALIGNING THE ORGANIZATION FOR ITS DIGITAL FUTURE.» *MIT Sloan Review.* 26 07. Accès le 07 2017. http://sloanreview.mit.edu/projects/aligning-for-digital-future/.

Goldman Sachs. 2014. «WHAT IS THE INTERNET OF THINGS?» *Goldman Sachs: Our thinking.* 09. Accès le 07 2017.

http://www.goldmansachs.com/our-thinking/pages/iot-infographic.html.

Greenough, John. 2014. «Business Insider UK.» 3 12. Accès le 07 2017. http://uk.businessinsider.com/four-elements-driving-iot-2014-10?r=US&IR=T.

Intel. s.d. «A guide to the Internet Of Things.» *Intel.com.* Accès le 07 2017. https://www.intel.com/content/www/us/en/internet-of-things/infographics/guide-to-iot.html.

John DeSarbo, ZS. 2015. «Rethinking Channel Strategy For The Internet Of Things.» *Channel Marketer Report.* 15 10. Accès le 07 2017. http://www.channelmarketerreport.com/2015/10/rethinking-channel-strategy-for-the-internet-of-things/.

Lineback, Rob. s.d. «The Market for Next-Generation Microsystems: More than MEMS.» Accès le 2017. http://www.powershow.com/view4/44aa36-ZGNjY/The_Market_for_Next-Generation_Microsystems_More_than_MEMS_powerpoint_ppt_presentation.

Lueth, Knud Lasse. 2014. «IoT Market – Forecasts at a glance.» *IoT Analytics.* 17 10. Accès le 07 14, 2017. https://iot-analytics.com/iot-market-forecasts-overview/.

MacGillivray, Carrie. 2016. «Worldwide Internet of Things Forecast Update, 2015-2019.» Report. https://www.idc.com/getdoc.jsp?containerId=US40983216.

Manusama, Michael Maoz | Jim Davies | Jenny Sussin | Olive Huang | Brian. 2016. «Predicts 2016: CRM Customer Service and Support.» *Gartner.* 24 08. Accès le 07 2017. https://www.gartner.com/doc/3168718/predicts--crm-customer-service.

marketsandmarkets.com. 2017. «Wi-Fi Chipset Market by IEEE Standards (802.11ay, 802.11ax, 802.11ac Wave 2), Band (Dual Band, Tri-Band), MIMO Configuration (SU-MIMO, MU-MIMO), Product Category (Smartphones, Tablets, PCS), and Geography - Global Forecast to 2022.» *marketsandmarkets.com.* 03. Accès le 07 2017. http://www.marketsandmarkets.com/Market-Reports/wi-fi-chipset-market-42186393.html.

MARTHA ZEMEDE, Keysight Technologies. 2015. «Building IoT gateways to the cloud.» *Microcontroller Tips.* 23 09. Accès le 07 2017. http://www.microcontrollertips.com/building-iot-gateways-to-the-cloud/.

McKinsey&Company. 2015. «THE INTERNET OF THINGS: MAPPING THE VALUE BEYOND THE HYPE.» *McKinsey&Company.* 06. Accès le 07 2017. https://www.mckinsey.de/files/unlocking_the_potential_of_the _internet_of_things_full_report.pdf.

Schmidbauer, Hardy. 2016. «NB-IoT vs LoRa Technology: which could take gold.» *Tracknet.io.* 09. Accès le 07 2017. http://tracknet.io/docs/LoRa-Alliance-Whitepaper_NBIoT_vs_LoRa.pdf.

Silicon Labs. s.d. «Battery Size Matters.» https://www.silabs.com/documents/public/white-papers/battery-life-in-connected-wireless-iot-devices.pdf.

Telefónica IoT Team. 2016. «16 facts you should know about the IoT in 2016.» *IOT GENERAL.* 29 01. Accès le 07 14, 2017. https://iot.telefonica.com/blog/16-facts-you-should-know-about-the-iot-in-2016.

U-Blox. 2017. «u-blox Short Range Modules.» *U-blox.com.* 30 06. Accès le 07 2017. https://www.u-blox.com/sites/default/files/u-blox-SHO-ATCommandsManual_(UBX-14044127).pdf.